Resistless Love:
Christian Witness in the New Millennium

(A Wesleyan Perspective)

S T Kimbrough, Jr.

GBGM Books
General Board of Global Ministries
The United Methodist Church
New York, NY

Resistless Love:
Christian Witness
in the New Millennium
(A Wesleyan Perspective)

Unless otherwise noted quotations from the Holy Bible are from the New Revised Standard Version Bible, copyright © 1989, by the Division of Christian Education of the National Council of the Churches of Christ in the United States of America.

S T Kimbrough, Jr., *Resistless Love: Christian Witness in the New Millennium (A Wesleyan Perspective)*
ISBN 1-890569-23-2

Cover design
Design Edge, Austin, Texas
Cover illustration
Shannon Faseler

Manufactured in the United States of America

This book is dedicated to the members of my immediate family, who have taught me the meaning of resistless love.

Contents

Part 3:

Personifying the Resistless Love of Jesus in the New Millennium

v

Preface

John Wesley bequeathed to later generations a distinctive understanding of the church whose primary mark is mission. Methodists were in mission before they became a church, and they became a church primarily for missional reasons. Methodists in general, and United Methodists in particular, should hail Kimbrough's new book as he projects the church's engagement in mission into a new century.

Resistless Love is not a rehash of what has gone before, but a Wesleyan-grounded vision of mission in a new time. It is a well-established fact that the Wesleyan perspective always entails the proclamation of the gospel as the heart of mission. Proclamation has various forms, and the usual interpretation of Wesley and his movement has focused on the verbal, spoken word of witness. Kimbrough clearly acknowledges Wesleyan tradition. Herein is found the vitally important contribution of this book. Taking his cue from Charles Wesley's poem about Elizabeth Blackwell (a participant in the Wesleyan revival) in which Charles writes, "[she] knows the stoutest to compel, / and sinners wins without the word," Kimbrough explores the role and power of the nonverbal witness of presence in the Wesleyan tradition. In the field of Wesleyan interpretation, Kimbrough is saying something new: A Wesleyan, holistic understanding of mission must conjoin the evangelical word with an evangelical presence.

James E. Logan
E. Stanley Jones Professor of Evangelism
Wesley Theological Seminary
Washington, D.C.

Part 1

Foundations of Christian Witness in the New Millennium

1. The Witness of Evangelical Word and Presence

As expressions of Christian communities' perception of their roles and reasons for existence, words like *witness, outreach, evangelism,* and *mission* evoke positive and negative responses. Across the centuries, the words have tended to draw the line between those who witness and those to whom one witnesses, those who reach out and those to whom one reaches out, between the evangelists and the evangelized, those who are on a mission and those who are the object of mission. There are those inside faith and its community and there are those who are outside both.

Central to the Christian faith are such concepts as love, peace, unity, justice, wholeness, and an ethic of doing "good to all, especially those of the family of faith" (Galatians 6:10). Yet, the Christian religion is perhaps the most fragmented and divided religion in the world. The self-perception of faith communities relies largely on denominational and confessional traditions whose priorities of initiation and membership become determinative for authentic identity. Yet historically, even these priorities become the source of discord, disunity, and divisiveness.

How can this religion of love possibly win the so-called "outsiders" over to a life of love, peace, wholeness, justice, and unity, when its own adherents cannot personify these concepts? Will the church intentionally move beyond denominationalism and be exemplary of these biblical ideas?

There is also the deeply negative influence of the violence and injustice which plague Christian history. The "outsiders" know this history well, and it impresses them too, though negatively. This is not the "good news" that Christians wish to proclaim. In many parts of the world today, the remnants and scars of colonialism still hinder the church's witness, because of the association of colonial power and the Christian church, especially where the missionaries recreated and

1

transplanted a "western" church at the expense of indigenous expressions of faith. If there is to be any hope for a life and mission of integrity in the Christian church of today and tomorrow, we must face the reality of this history, while not brooding upon it.

It is perhaps easy to stand within a Christian communion and never really see the way those outside it perceive Christians. It is a natural reflex to disclaim responsibility for the bad chapters of Christian history with a resounding, "It is not my fault. Those were obviously misguided and deluded individuals." But for those who claim to be followers of Jesus, the history of Christians and the church must be claimed as "our history," the good and the bad.

The church's history is a long story of "us" and the "others," and this polarity is not limited to the community of faith's insiders and outsiders but also permeates the faith community or church.

The violence and injustice practiced in the name of Christ and the church throughout the last 2,000 years make one ask how the church today dare evangelize others in the name of love, God's love revealed in Jesus Christ. The early church councils showed signs of growing tensions within the church out of which eventually emerged divisions and schisms. The "top-down evangelism" whereby monarchs and other rulers from Constantine to Vladimir declared their subjects to be Christian produced questionable results. The first major division of the church into the Roman Catholic Church and the Orthodox churches of the East foreshadowed church divisions to follow. The slaughters by the Crusaders in the "Holy War" to conquer the "holy places" of the "Holy Land" for Christ and the church revealed the power struggles of ecclesiastical and governmental hierarchies that continue to plague the church and hinder its witness to the present day. The horrors of the Spanish Inquisition and persecution of nonconformists in the name of legalism and morality remain a major stumbling block to Christian witness in many parts of the world. The mistaken fusion of monarchical thrones and priestly offices has left generations marked with confusion and despair about what and who the church really is.

The abuses that precipitated the Reformation were by no means the monopoly of Rome. Rather, they prefigured injustices which would characterize almost every subsequent offshoot of the Christian religion. Each new group wants to *begin again* with the hope that it will not repeat the errors of the past, and, hence, a plethora of churches and sects are now spread across the world. Are these the children of unity and concord? Are these the ones who have had their lives reclaimed by the love of Jesus, who live by such imperatives as "Love your enemy," "Love your neighbor as yourself," and "Love the Lord your God with all your heart, soul, mind, and strength"? How fervently Christians have sung the hymn "Onward, Christian Soldiers" and proclaimed "We are not divided, all one body we." Is that a fact?

There can be no question that story after story can be told of followers of Jesus who personified his love in thought, word, and deed. There were St. Francis of Assisi, Albert Schweizer, Mother Teresa, and others who emulated a spirit of life-giving love and service. And, as stated above, followers of Jesus must claim both the good and the bad of the church's history. There is a tendency, however, to dwell upon the latter at the expense of the former.

It is important to seek a balanced historical perspective. Claiming the positive aspects of Christian history is vital to contemporary and future Christian witness. Obsession with one period of history and its injustices leads to a warped understanding of Christianity. There are seekers and doers of justice in every age, as well as those who promote and practice justice. Christian witness in the new millennium cannot afford a one-sided view of the past. It is much too easy to view the Crusades, the Spanish Inquisition, and European colonialism as the main realities of the Christian religion. Dr. Dana Robert, however, appropriately points out, "The age of Colonialism is a mere blip on the screen in the longer history of Christianity."[1] This may also be said of the Crusades and the Spanish Inquisition.

Dr. Samuel Hugh Moffett in his *History of Christianity in Asia* offers an important historical corrective by telling the story of Christianity in the East which is not as well known as the story of Christianity in the West. It is the same gospel that is preached and lived, "But it was sown by different sowers; it was planted in different soil; it grew with a different flavor; it was gathered by different reapers."[2] Moffett reveals effective indigenization of the Christian faith throughout Asia, as well as cultural clashes that emerged with the spread of Christianity. As the church seeks today to equip indigenous leadership, it will find important lessons and guidance in Moffett's work that are foundational for this endeavor.

What message has the world received from the spread of Christianity and its churches?

The prophet Isaiah cries out to the children of Israel, "Who has believed our report?" (Isaiah 53:1). Christians are asked anew in every age who will believe the report of a people of God who seek to live and love as Jesus did? What does history teach us that we should believe? Do we simply ignore the past 2,000 years of church history and return to the world of the Old and New Testaments to find meaning? "To your tents, O Israel," (1 Kings 12:16) is the cry of the people of Israel to King Rehoboam, who would not listen to their pleas. They thought if they could just return to the days of King David, things would be better.

From within the church, such assertions are relatively easy to make. But the "outsiders" will not let the "insiders" so easily exercise historical amnesia. Too many monarchs and "princes" of the church have plundered the rich and pillaged the poor. Too many "believers" have idly ignored or energetically condoned confiscation of property, imprisonment and enslavement of the innocent, denial of human rights, cross burnings, lynchings, and exploitation of the poor and needy. At the same time the church is often guilty of historical amnesia in not revealing and telling its story of the fullness, richness, and goodness of its witness.

It is ironic that the United States of America was founded on a constitution that maintains all people are created equal and are entitled to certain inalienable rights (life, liberty, and the pursuit of happiness) when its establishment was made possible through the tribal extinction and death of millions of Native Americans, as well as the blood and sweat of African-American slaves. Almost a century would pass from the 1776 Declaration of Independence to Abraham Lincoln's Emancipation Proclamation! The story of the opponents of slavery, including faithful Christian leaders, such as John Wesley, Charles Wesley, and William Wilberforce, is also a vital part of this history and Christian witness.

Are then the truths of God's redemptive and healing love lost forever in the ruins of evil and injustice? No, there is "Good News" to proclaim! Christian truth, lifestyle, and witness must not be so shaped by negative historical realities that the true realities of God's love revealed in Jesus have no possibility of acknowledgment? As evangels of the gospel today what shall we proclaim? How shall we live the gospel of love? Where do we begin?

Repentance

Any gospel proclamation of the present and future must begin with repentance. There is no gospel to proclaim without repentance first. It is not the repentance of those to whom the gospel is proclaimed that is meant here but the repentance of the proclaimers. Those who would proclaim with their words and their lives the gospel of redeeming love must publicly acknowledge their participation in the sinful heritage and history of the Christian religion. It is only then that authentic witness of word and deed can begin. Perhaps the following statement by Paul is the most mature preface to the church's and the Christian's witness in any age: "I am the foremost" of sinners (1 Timothy 1:15). Inheritors of the gospel stand not only in the lineage of Jesus and all the prophets and wise ones who preceded him, but in the lineage of all who have claimed his name, past and present.

The purpose of such repentance is not to create a perpetual Christian guilt complex, but to acknowledge historical realities and realize that a proclamation of gospel truth cannot be authentic unless prefaced by open repentance. To profess, proclaim, and live a perfecting love is laughable without repentance. The church since its inception has been corrupt, for its members are human beings. The Bible from beginning to end describes the reality of what it means to be fallible. The children of creation have an incredible capacity for good and evil. They are loving and hateful, gentle and violent, selfish and selfless. They make war and peace in an unending cycle. They kill and maim and give birth and care for the sick.

Proclaim as they may the gospel of Jesus Christ, Christians can only make the message of redemptive love viable if they proclaim it with their lives. Walter Bruggemann eloquently declares: "Evangelism cannot be a program strategy, but a revolutionary way of enacting the hope and energy of the believing community."[3]

Great Commission/Great Commandment

Historically, the church has not always found it easy to reconcile the Great Commission of Jesus, "Go therefore and make disciples of all nations, baptizing in the name of the Father, and of the Son, and of the Holy Spirit," (Matthew 28:19) and his Great Commandment, "Love one another. Just as I have loved you, you also should love one another" (John 13:34).

As one reads the history of the church, one might think that many who were zealous to proclaim the gospel saw the Great Commission as the Great Commandment: namely, that nothing can be more important than proclaiming God's Good News of salvation in Jesus Christ, especially to those who have never heard it. This is the highest calling and Christ's greatest mandate to the church. The results of such a perspective in evangelism have not always produced loving realities or expressions of the Great Commandment. The stories of cultural, economic, and societal subjugation by the missionary enterprise are no secret.

This writer finds it an absolute wonder that so many Native Americans are Christians today. The wonder is not that they find in the gospel of Jesus Christ the full expression of divine love which renews life and gives it full meaning, but rather that those who brought them the gospel of love obliterated their tribes and drove them from their homes and lands. This is not to say that there were not among the early settlers some who were opposed to such horrible deeds, but they were not the dominant force in dealing with the Native Americans.

What if, in the history of Christian mission, the Great Commandment to love all of God's creatures and creation itself had been as important as the Great Commission? Might the spiritual landscape of North America be different today?

What if early missionaries to Africa had not viewed drums as instruments of heathen music and culture but had lovingly encouraged the first African Christians to develop Christian song out of their own rhythms, music, and language? Would we have had to wait so long for the emergence of indigenous African Christian song? What if the Great Commandment to love others, indeed to love others as God has made them, had dominated the missionary enterprise of the church? Of course, there were always those who loved because God loved, but they were often in the minority.

One thing, however, that is often overlooked in the historical evaluation of the western missionary enterprise's "transplantation" of western culture and mores is that the missionaries themselves were often part of a subculture in the western lands from which they came. They were not necessarily the stalwart representatives of western culture one might expect. They often stood in opposition to the cultures from which they came and sought to create a life that would not duplicate the "worst" of their own world. In seeking to recreate the biblical world, which was immersed in the thought and life of the ancient Near East, they often acted without due regard for how the gospel message would resonate among different cultures and peoples. If the Great Commandment had always been held in as high esteem in theory and practice as the Great Commission, the history of Christian missions would have been quite different.

Is this then a mere plea for acculturated Christianity? No! But the gospel of God's love in Christ does not resonate the same way everywhere in the world, and one must be open to the movement of God's Spirit among all peoples and cultures, for they are a vital part of God's diverse creation. Did God make mistakes in the creation of human and cultural diversity? No! Human beings make mistakes in misunderstanding the glory of God's marvelously varied creation. This diversity must be honored and loved, though not idolized.

There is a danger, however, in making the cultural attachment of Christianity its reason for being. When religion becomes identified primarily with ethnicity and culture, one slowly begins to breed exclusivism, particularism, and enmity. Nothing could be more contrary to the Christian gospel message. *The Great Commission may give universal voice to the gospel, but it is the Great Commandment that gives it universal resonance.*

If the love passages of holy scripture literally became the heartbeat of those who seek to follow Christ and his way, what a transformation the church would experience worldwide. What if Christ's followers really (1) loved their neighbors as themselves, (2) loved their enemies, (3) exercised enough love to lay down their lives for their friends, (4) were long-suffering in love, and (5) endured all things in love?

If the gospel has been preached and not been lived in love, one has missed the whole point of the gospel. We shall explore, therefore, in this volume what this author calls "witnessing with your life." It mandates an embodiment and personification of the Great Commandment. While the Great Commandment is no substitute for the Great Commission, it is in the living out of Christ's self-giving love that we discover that we have proclaimed the gospel, even when we did not know we were doing so.

Witnessing with a Life of Resistless Love

To speak of nonverbal evangelism would seem to be a contradiction in terms, for does not evangelism have to do with the proclamation of the gospel of Jesus Christ and imply a verbal process? If one is going to articulate anything about the redemptive message of Jesus, does this not require the use of words? And does not Matthew 28 mandate that followers of Jesus Christ proclaim his message to the ends of the earth? Yet Charles Wesley suggests in his poem about Elizabeth Blackwell, wife of a noted London banker, that she proclaimed God's Good News in Christ and never uttered a word. Others came to their faith in Christ through the power of the gospel she lived. This by no means is to suggest that words of proclamation are not significant. Rather it is to affirm that the Holy Scriptures make extremely clear that verbal proclamation is not the only way to articulate God's redemptive love and draw people to Christ. Note how Wesley shapes the idea of witnessing with one's life, as he writes about Elizabeth Blackwell:

> By wisdom pure and peaceable,
>   by the meek Spirit of her Lord,
> she knows the stoutest to compel,
>   and sinners wins without a word:
> they see the tempers of the Lamb,
>   and bow subdued to Jesu's name,
> as captives of resistless love.

Here we come to the title of this book, *Resistless Love*. The author means that "resistless love" is at the heart of "Christian witness in the new millennium." It encompasses what is sometimes referred to as "mission evangelism," namely: *the proclamation of the gospel of Jesus Christ through the full spectrum of mission in all one is, says, thinks, and does.*

What we wish to explore in this book are images and avenues of witnessing through resistless love that are affirmed in the Scriptures, often by Jesus himself, and how they may become viable for Christians in any age and place. This is not an easy task, for to utter the word "evangelism" evokes a mental picture of someone, usually male, standing before a crowd of people declaring in some language the story of God's Good News. Charles Wesley affirms in the above text what scripture is ever saying: resistless love evangelizes! Let it be stated here once again, however, that this inquiry does not propose an alternative to traditional verbal evangelism. What it does is maintain that verbal and nonverbal evangelism are not alternatives but parts of a larger whole, namely, the vocation of the evangel, who articulates in thought, word, and action the viability and effectiveness of God's love. This means that words alone can never suffice for the vocation of the evangel, which is the vocation of every follower of Jesus. Whether or not one has the gift of words, one is to articulate God's redemptive, healing, saving love as one comes to experience it in a self-giving Jesus, and one must exude this love from the very core of one's being so that others will be drawn by the same power of love. This means that all are called in Christ to the vocation of love. We are called to articulate God's loving message by so living that it is unquestionably clear to all that God's love is the empowering and guiding force in our lives. Such love is irresistible, or in Charles Wesley's wording—"resistless."

There is a basic difference between verbal and nonverbal evangelism. One is very aware when one is engaged in verbal evangelism, for one is either uttering the words of Good News or hearing them spoken. One knows when one is evangelizing or being evangelized. That is not always the case, however, when one witnesses through resistless love. One does not always know who is responding to one's action, body language, glance, touch, or openness and the effect it is having on others.

If one follows Jesus through the gospels of the New Testament, it is interesting to note how differently he deals with people from the way the church has traditionally dealt with others in its evangelism. Of course, Jesus uses words and tells stories and parables, but the power of his effectiveness lies in the way he personifies the love of which he speaks in all that he is and does. He is God's love in action, whether speaking or not. It is here that we find an important clue and key to witnessing through resistless love. The evangel personifies God's Good News of redemptive love. The life of the evangel constantly poses a question to others — "Will you follow the same Christ who can make you love?"

Albert Outler summons all to consider the evangelistic power of the visible word in his book *Evangelism in the Wesleyan Spirit*.

> My point is that evangelism must issue in visible social effects or else its fruits will fade and wither. Christian proclamation must take on visible form and the Christian community must be committed to social reform, or else it will stultify our Lord's prayer that God's righteous will shall be done *on earth*—here and now, in justice and love and peace—as always it is being done in heaven. Outward witness in daily living is the necessary confirmation of any inward experience of inward faith. The Word made *audible* must become the Word made *visible*, if . . . lives are ever to be touched by the "Word made flesh."[4]

What Outler says has been illuminated by feminist theologians in our time who emphasize that it is not only the content of the proclamation that is important but also the location. The historical exclusion of women from the pulpit has led them in different directions in evangelism. "Women have often circumvented the power centers of evangelism and have evangelized in an informal setting, often around a table. The table as a place for proclamation coincides with the table as an image of God's reign and its concomitant social reintegration."[5]

Furthermore, liberation theology has stressed from new perspectives the Wesleyan emphasis that conversion involves a twofold "turning"—away from and toward. It is personal and social. It cannot be one or the other. Conversion evokes changes in individuals and in the world in which they find themselves. When Charles Wesley wrote the line "Help us to make the poor our friends," he was issuing a call to social reintegration around the table, for we invite our friends to our table. The commitment of one's life to Jesus Christ is a commitment of one's life to others—to neighbor, to stranger, to friend.

The witness of resistless love is a call to social reintegration around the table, and this is the reason why for the Wesleys and for the church in the future, the witness of the "table of all tables," the table of Holy Communion, becomes evangelization. The Wesleys saw it as indeed the place where God's resistless love enables the social reintegration of all peoples for all time and space.

Where shall we turn for images, metaphors, and models of witnessing through resistless love? Without question evangelism is concerned traditionally with proclaiming the Good News of God's love that others may come to know the saving grace of that love in the life, death, and resurrection of Jesus Christ. But the Scriptures make very clear that words are not the only way in which this knowledge is imparted or becomes a part of human experience. Jesus expressed it in this way:

> Beware of false prophets, who come to you in sheep's clothing but inwardly are ravenous wolves. You will know them by their fruits. Are grapes gathered from thorns or figs from thistles? In the same way, every good tree bears good fruit, but the bad tree bears bad fruit. A good tree cannot bear bad fruit, nor can a bad tree bear good fruit. Every tree that does not bear good fruit is cut down and thrown into the fire. Thus, you will know them by their fruit. (Matthew 15:17–20)

The fruit of our lives is how others know who we are. This is how they know whom we follow and, hence, what makes up the essence of our being. The fruit that the lives of Christian evangels bear is "love fruit." God sows the seed of love within us and we bear the fruit, the "love fruit."

How we perceive love is crucial to an understanding of witnessing through resistless love, and if we are to bear its fruit, we must have a clear vision of love's meaning as we come to understand it through God's revelation in Jesus Christ.

Before turning to the multiple nonverbal ways in which we witness to resistless love with our lives, let us consider the importance of witnessing to it with words, for our word witness is fundamental to love witness.

2. *The Witness of the Word and Words*

Witnessing to the Good News of the redemptive love of Jesus Christ is generally word-oriented. The word which became flesh is constantly articulated, proclaimed, and explained in words. Yet, the very incarnation of Jesus Christ as God's own child was a wordless event. It was a birth event, an act of divine intervention. Indeed, according to the New Testament, it was announced by the words of prophets and the heavenly hosts. But the Incarnation itself, the becoming flesh of the word, was not a verbally bound event. God acted and became incarnate. The divine *logos,* word, was articulated in human form. The heavenly hosts acclaimed the birth of the Savior, and an angel announced the coming birth to Mary. The announcement, recorded in scripture, is commonly known as the Annunciation and was followed by Mary's joyful response known as the *Magnificat* or *Song of Mary.*

To speak of the incarnate word with words is perhaps a very natural thing, given the reality that words are a major means of human communication and that Christ himself left his followers with the mandate to proclaim the gospel.

While much of this volume addresses the reality of evangelizing in multiple ways without words, it is important in this chapter to address the indispensability of the witness that issues from the spoken word. It is difficult to overemphasize the vital nature of proclaiming the word with words! This should not be done, however, at the expense of other modes of effective witnessing, many of which are addressed here.

The Divine Word

Let us consider first what the Scriptures say regarding the divine word, the word which transcends all human words, the word which communicates itself in spite of human words.

The prophet Isaiah emphasized the *eternal nature of the word,*

God's own means of communicating divine will, way, and love. "The grass withers, the flower fades, but the word of God will stand for ever" (40:8). The word of God is couched in the words of holy scripture, but it existed before the Scriptures were ever written. It is more than words, phrases, sentences, and books. It transcends all of these. God's word was expressed in every act of creation and continues to be expressed in ongoing creation. The Holy Scriptures are unquestionably God's word to humankind, but God had a will, a way, an expression of love that preceded the written word. These precipitated the word expressed in holy scripture. Hence, the word of God in the words of scripture takes on even stronger authenticity as the revelation of God's preexistent word.

The eternal nature of this enduring word is emphasized in the Gospel of Luke, "Heaven and earth will pass away, but my words will not pass away" (21:33). And the Gospel of John stresses that the word was "in the beginning" (1:1). God articulates this eternal word in the Holy Scriptures and there we learn that it "became flesh and lived among us" (John 1:14).

If one accepts the eternal and enduring nature of the word of God that has expressed itself among God's people in the temple, the church, and the synagogue, then one might expect that the community of the faithful would willingly follow its truth and teaching. But that is far from the reality revealed in the Holy Scriptures. When approached by the Pharisees and scribes about why his disciples broke "the tradition of the elders" by not washing their hands before they ate (Matthew 15:2), Jesus made a very significant reply. After an explanation of how the Pharisees and scribes hedged the commandment to "Honor your father and mother," he said, "So, for the sake of your tradition, you make void the word of God. You hypocrites! Isaiah prophesied rightly about you when he said: 'This people honors me with their lips, but their hearts are far from me; in vain do they worship me, teaching human precepts as doctrine'" (Matthew 15:6–9). Is it possible for evangelists to do lip service to the gospel and have their hearts miss the core of the message?

When one considers the vast number of Christian churches in the world that proclaim the word of God passionately in their own way, is it possible that one's own tradition of proclaiming the word, of witnessing, of evangelizing, could make void the word of God? Can all ways and methods be authentic and valid? Think of the manifold approaches and practices: witness through word-oriented liturgy and sacrament, through word-oriented evangelistic crusades, through word-oriented spiritual laws and evangelical doctrinal prescriptions to which adherence is expected (if not required), word-oriented prayers and Bible studies designed to evoke a specific response. And, of course, there are many other master plans that provide a checklist for whether evangelism *really* has been done. How shall we know the truth about the authentic proclamation of the word of God? Is the only valid proclamation of the word one that offers with each spoken proclamation "the plan of salvation"?

Qualities of the Divine Word

There are many qualities of the word of God in the Holy Scriptures. *It is a guide:* "Your word is a lamp to my feet and a light to my path" (Psalm 119:105). The word also has *a magnetic power* all its own that draws people to it. At the time of the early church, "the word of God continued to advance and gain adherents" (Acts 12:24).

As much as some might wish to believe that they have a special dispensation to proclaim the word, that, indeed, they have a unique claim upon it in terms of interpretation and tradition, Paul's affirmation in 2 Timothy 2:9 is worthy of keen attention: *"The word of God is not chained"* or bound. Its freedom is God's, not that of humankind.

Yet another quality of God's word is emphasized in the Book of Hebrews: "the word of God is *living and active,* sharper than any two-edged sword . . . It is able to judge the thoughts and intentions of the heart" (4:12). The word of God itself has a living quality—it is not a dead word, though it comes from ancient times so far as biblical revelation is concerned. It is alive! It tells all who will hear, all who will listen, all who will respond, how to live motivated and sustained by self-giving, resistless love, as shown by Jesus on the cross.

When Paul wrote to the church at Colossae, he also illuminated another quality of the word: *it indwells the followers of Christ,* the word made flesh. "Let the word of Christ dwell in you richly; teach and admonish one another in all wisdom; and with gratitude in your hearts sing psalms, hymns, and spiritual songs to God" (Colossians 3:16). The word of Christ, which is all-encompassing, selfless love, so enriches life that we teach and admonish each other in wisdom, and gratitude fills our hearts to the extent that our faith bursts into song. If we love the Christ who imbues life with these dimensions of human relationships, we will follow the word of God. From Jesus' own words we learn, "Those who love me will keep my words, and my Father will love them, and we will come to them and make our home with them" (John 14:23). Small wonder that Charles Wesley, one of the founders of the Methodist movement in eighteenth-century England, should aver that we become "transcripts of the Trinity," ones in whom Father, Son, and Holy Spirit dwell in full relationship, which expresses itself in incarnated, Spirit-filled, resistless love to all with whom the followers of Christ come in contact.

The Human Word

In the Hebrew and Greek Scriptures, the importance of words, written, read, and spoken in private and in corporate worship, is emphasized. The psalmist deeply wants to speak only words that are acceptable to God. "Let the words of my mouth and the meditation of my heart be acceptable to you, O Lord, my rock and redeemer" (19:14). *Speaking words "acceptable" to God* then is vital for the believer and the community of faith, and determinative for Christian witness. It is not enough to speak just any word or to speak thoughtlessly. Words give evidence of one's own faith commitment, not only to others but to God.

What issues from the mouth of those who claim to be members of the household of faith determines the effectiveness of their witness. The history of the Christian church reveals that it has not always been easy for Christians to *speak the appropriate word* for the witness of the gospel. The admonition of the Book of Proverbs, however, should always be applied to evangelism methods: "A word fitly spoken is like apples of gold in a setting of silver" (25:11).

The Book of Ecclesiastes adjures everyone: "Never be rash with your mouth, nor let your heart be quick to utter a word before God, for God is in heaven, and you upon earth; therefore let your words be few" (5:2). *Economy of words* should also be a characteristic of

Christian evangelism.

When Jesus said in the Gospel of Matthew, "I tell you, on the day of judgment you will have to give account for every careless word you utter; for by your words you will be justified, and by your words you will be condemned" (12:36–37), he uttered words which are to be applied to evangelism, though they are often thought more commonly to apply to one's responsibility for personal behavior. Since, however, we are speaking here of the use of words to proclaim the gospel, the question of *careless words* is of utmost importance.

Witnessing with Words in the New Millennium

Our world has changed radically in the last half of the twentieth century. Sound bites circling the world through cyberspace, instantaneous translations of almost any language, picture images which flash across television screens providing visual history in the making, and hosts of other technical communication developments make our words on behalf of the gospel crucial to effective witness and Christian lifestyle.

As the English translation of the German chorale "O Haupt voll Blut und Wunden" ("O Sacred Head now wounded") asks in stanza three, "What language shall I borrow / to thank thee, dearest friend?" so too we ask as we consider proclaiming the gospel in the new millennium: What language shall we use to articulate to others the saving and redemptive love of God in Jesus Christ that surpasses all other loves? The formulas and methods are innumerable and some would say that it is quite sufficient simply to quote holy scripture.

We, like the author of the text of the German chorale, should be totally awestruck as we consider the enormous task of being stewards of God's word and its message. Like Charles Wesley in the first line of his conversion hymn, we should ask: "Where shall my wondering soul begin?" Any proclamation of the gospel that does not begin with such humility is destined to miss the mark. Here is the beginning point for the use of all words to proclaim the word—come to the task with humility realizing the inadequacy of words to articulate God's ultimate reality.

Of primary importance is the context within which one speaks. This does not mean that we change what the Scriptures say about the need for the acknowledgment of sin, repentance, and commitment of one's life to a self-giving love in Jesus Christ. But it does mean we learn to speak with keen sensitivities.

Our world has become a melting pot of human ethnicities and cultures, and almost anywhere one goes one finds a pluralistic culture, even among diverse tribal groups within delimited areas of the two-thirds world. Cultural sensitivity becomes a vital aspect of proclaiming the gospel and of how it resonates with people. Mercy Amba Oduyoye, the distinguished Ghanaian theologian, reminds those who want to speak of the heart as the center of human emotion and spirituality that this will not resonate well with the Akan people of Ghana, whose mode of expression for the seat of human emotions is captured in the word "bowels." So to speak of "turning one's *heart* to Jesus" may have little meaning for the Akan.

Those who would witness effectively in the new millennium must exhibit keen sensitivity to multicultural, multiethnic, multireligious, and multilingual contexts. The history of mission is filled with examples that underscore the need for these sensitivities.

In India, violence has sometimes erupted between Hindus and Christians in areas where tribal peoples who have converted to Christianity have been encouraged by Christian mentors to continue tilling the soil at a time when a certain Hindu tradition understands the earth to be in a menstrual cycle and unfit for cultivation until its period passes. To disregard such tradition and essentially say by one's actions as a Christian that others who adhere to it are heathen idiots is the height of cultural insensitivity and religious arrogance. This has no place in witnessing to God's word.

In proclaiming the word of God in diverse religious contexts, one must be as diligent a student of other religions as one is of the Christian faith. For example, show respect for the Qur'an among Muslim friends. Read it as a holy book, not as heathen doggerel. Know it as well as you know the Bible. In a Buddhist context, know that simply speaking of a Creator is relatively meaningless, for there is no role for the Creator in Buddhism. Cling passionately to the Christian faith, but respect these differences.

As the worlds of science, cyberspace, outer space, and inner space (spirituality) approach one another and find common concerns for human and ecological survival, language is the vital means by which the gaps of mistrust, misunderstanding, and ignorance can be bridged. Hence, John Wesley's commitment to universal knowledge, which imbues the Christian with an unswerving and undying passion for learning, must be a part of Christian witness in the twenty-first century. Wesley understood that, as a child of creation, one must grasp as much of its wonder as possible. His concern to make subjects like medicine, geography, world history, and science accessible to all is foundational for effective witness to the gospel. Therefore, maintain an insatiable appetite for learning!

The most difficult task facing Christians intent on proclaiming the gospel in the new millennium is how to include others in the message proclaimed and lived. Evangelism has often tended to draw the line between the "insiders" and "outsiders," the "saved" and the "unsaved." But in terms of the biblical message, there are no outsiders. God chose to give the divine Son in redeeming, self-emptying love for *all people,* and *all creation.* No one is excepted. Christ died and rose for all! *The gospel is genuinely, truly, and wholly inclusive!* There is neither Jew nor Greek, male nor female, bond nor free. And this applies globally to all dimensions of church and community. Regardless of gender or age, all have been claimed by God in Christ before they ever consider responding positively or negatively to this claim.

We continue to follow the mandate of our God to speak the Good News of salvation indeed because there are those who have not heeded and those who have not heard. The message is that God has included all in this plan of redemptive love, and Christian proclamation must be a message of loving acceptance of all peoples as they are. Does this mean that there is no choice, no human freedom in the decision to follow God's accepting love? Universal salvation with no human accountability is not the message of scripture. Human beings are accountable to God and one another for their response to God's summons to accept the self-emptying love of Christ as the redemptive, saving power in their lives and to personify such love. It is clear from the violence, death, greed, and power mongering in today's world that thousands choose the road to destruction, rejecting God's claim of love on their lives, rather than accept selfless, resistless love on a cross that saves the world from condemnation and the road to hell engineered by sin, hatred, and war. The clarion call of scripture to all people remains: "Choose this day whom you will serve" (Joshua 24:15).

Yes, the message is a decisive word and the Bible teaches the kind of love that is the most powerful force in earth and heaven. Recently a friend in an Asian country where Christianity is a minority religion said that converts were multiplying daily because the people saw that Christians really loved and cared for one another and were truly concerned for each other's well-being.

The proclaimers of the word must indeed choose words carefully, for words proclaimed and not lived will destroy the witness of the gospel. They must choose appropriate or fitting words and choose them economically.

Cruciform Witness of the Word in the New Millennium

It is in the cross of Jesus Christ that one discovers the key posture for the witness of the word in the new millennium. What does it mean to say that Christian witness should be cruciform? The idea of a cross-shaped or cruciform witness suggests that such witness should bear the imprint or shape of the cross. Word witness must be self-emptying and self-giving. It must be a pouring out of oneself in love for others, just as Jesus did for all people in all ages. It cannot be self-serving or self-aggrandizing. It has one purpose—to awaken the world to redeeming, reclaiming, sacrificial love, of which the world is in such desperate need.

If proclaimers of the word will look to the cross, they will find in Jesus' demeanor and in his words important examples of cruciform witness.

Cruciform witness always expresses a concern for others. Even in his agony, Jesus looked down upon his mother and compassionately expressed his concern for her. "When Jesus saw his mother, and the disciple whom he loved [John] standing near, he said to his mother, 'Woman, behold, your son!' Then he said to the disciple, 'Behold, your mother!'" As he died, he thought of his own mother's emptiness and loss and that of his beloved follower (John 19:26–27).

The witness of the word must always be filled with a sense of compassion and concern for others and their relationships. This must be determinative for every word chosen to proclaim the gospel.

Cruciform witness is marked by human vulnerability. When Jesus speaks the words, "I am thirsty" (John 19:28), the human vulnerability of the Son of God is nowhere more apparent in the New Testament than here. He is a child of God and a child of earth. He feels our pain and knows what it is to thirst.

Those who hear the witness of the word must sense human vulnerability in the bearer of the Good News. It is not incidental that St. Paul said, "My strength is made perfect in weakness " (2 Corinthians 12:9, KJV). A helpful prayer before or after a minister of the gospel proclaims the word is, "O God, bless the gospel that has been preached, correct the errors of my interpretation and confirm the truth therein."

Cruciform witness is imbued with forgiveness. Jesus' words, "Father, forgive them; for they do not know what they are doing," (Luke 23:24) point to the defining posture of witness of the word. It is forgiving! And Christian behavior must match the message! In colonial America, a Native American chief responded to a colonial government official, who was adjuring the chief and his tribe to convert to Christianity, that when he and his people saw the Christians, who had killed and maimed them, practice the love and forgiveness which they preached, they would become Christians. Cruciform witness must be matched by a cruciform life of self-emptying, forgiving, resistless love. Let the witness of the word always be a forgiving word.

Cruciform witness is the promise of full union with God. Jesus said to one of the thieves, "Truly I tell you, today you will be with me in Paradise" (Luke 23:43). The word from God is a word of promise and hope. While *paradise* has often been thought of as a prize for the repentant sinner, it is the promise of union with God, "today you will be with me," that the world is open to hearing. There is a hunger for spirituality—for encounter and union with God. *Cruciform witness affirms the promise of the fulfillment of our spiritual journey with God.* It is a promise of hope in life, in death, and beyond death.

Cruciform witness commits everything to God—especially the words and the word. Jesus sets the tone for this dimension of witness when he says, "Father, into your hands I commend my spirit" (Luke 23:46). Can you commend your word witness to God? This is a question every Christian must constantly ask. Is my witness of the word, witness to the word, commendable to God? This will place in focus what we say, to whom we say it, and when and where we say it. Can we and do we speak the word that is "acceptable" in God's sight, who alone is our strength and redeemer.

Finally, there is another dimension of Christ's Calvary experience that should not be overlooked in the witness of the word. He went to his death boldly and without timidity, in spite of his agony in the Garden of Gethsemane over the cup of suffering and death. Take his example as a pattern for the witness of the word. Let self-examination, even agonizing self-examination and prayer, preface word witness. Then proclaim the word boldly and without timidity! Proclaim the message of sin, repentance, and God's forgiveness forthrightly and with passion. No world has been in greater need of healing, redemptive love than today's world.

Christ has died! Christ has risen! Christ will come again! This same Christ heals brokenness and alienation with the love that excels all other loves.

Let Christ's cruciform life shape your witness of the word!

3. The Witness of Resistless Love

The meaning of the word *love* does not begin in the New Testament. It has a lengthy history in the Holy Scriptures. The Hebrew word *ahavat* appears on page after page of the Hebrew Scriptures. There people love one another, express their love for God, and God loves them. The New Testament has no monopoly on the word *love,* nor did Jesus invent it!

Certainly many of the nuances of the Hebrew word are distributed among the three Greek words for *love* in the New Testament: *eros, philos, agape*. But regardless of the nuances which identify various dimensions of human and divine love in the Holy Scriptures (Hebrew and Greek), why is it that the communities of the faithful who claim to base their personal and corporate life upon the Scriptures have never been able to personify a love that unites them as a healing force in the world? Judaism and Christianity remain divided within themselves, as other living faiths that draw strength from the Holy Scriptures remain divided within themselves and are at best only fragmented examples of holistic, unifying, healing love. Who has actualized these admonitions: "You shall love the Lord your God with all your heart, and with all your soul, and with all your mind," (Matthew 22:37) and "You shall love your neighbor as yourself" (Leviticus 19:18)?

It is easy to excuse the faith community's failure by proclaiming the universality of sin, which is proven daily in a world still held captive by power, greed, and war. But this is much too facile a claim, for it does not test at all the viability of the love vision of the scriptures as a truly possible, livable reality.

Could it be that the failure of the faith community to personify the love vision of the Bible lies in the fact that this vision is not the model of outreach, focus, and lifestyle of such a community?

It shall be the task here to focus on the church as a community of those who seek to be faithful to the gospel and who claim both the Hebrew and Greek Scriptures as the foundation for community life, purpose, and witness. Nevertheless one must ask, Why is a body of people that claims to draw its strength from the love of Jesus as the model for personal and corporate life one of the most divided bodies in the entire world? Why is the history of the Christian church filled with avarice, power struggles, intimidation, malice, and the taking of life? Why should anyone believe that this is a community of love?

How did the holistic, prophetic vision of Deuteronomy, "You shall love the Lord your God with all your heart, and with all your soul, and with all your mind," and the priestly vision of Leviticus, "You shall love your neighbor as yourself," become secondary for the religious community? Is it a wonder that Paul, a Jew by birth and education, should claim in his celebrated 13th chapter of 1 Corinthians that "faith, hope, and love abide, these three, but the greatest of these is love"? Any faithful Jew should have believed that.

Has the church reversed the order and claimed that the most important is faith? Is St. Paul wrong? Church history would seem to affirm that he was. To see this, one need only review the most important church councils, the Crusades, and the continued priority in many arenas that the church places upon possessing and affirming a faith that meets specific language tests, be these doctrinal or liturgical. It is precisely this which St. Paul indicted, when he declared that the eloquence of angels to disclose the most elusive mysteries would be futile, if we had not love. *Love has ultimate priority,* says St. Paul.

How does one view life both as it is and as it ought to be? Consider the words of Cervantes in the musical *Man of La Mancha:*

> I have lived nearly fifty years, and I have seen life as it is. Pain, misery, hunger . . . cruelty beyond belief. I have heard the singing from taverns and the moans from bundles of filth on the streets. I have been a soldier and seen my comrades fall in battle . . . or die more slowly under the lash in Africa. I have held them in my arms at the final moment. These were men who saw life as it is, yet they died despairing. No glory, no gallant last words . . . only their eyes filled with confusion, whimpering the question: "Why?" I do not think they asked why they were dying, but why they had lived.

When life itself seems lunatic, who knows where madness lies? Too much sanity may be madness. To seek
treasure where there is only trash. Perhaps to be practical
is madness. And maddest of all is to see life as it is and
not as it ought to be.[1]

What is your vision of life as it is and as what it ought to be? You
know why you are dying—you are mortal and cannot avoid it. But
what about why you are *living*? Does love witness to what your life
is and what it ought to be? Is love, God's love, the reason for your
life? Does it keep you going from day to day?

With the advent of each new year come the questions: What
abides? What endures? Some of us have lost loved ones during the
past year. Many have lost their homes and possessions to the ravages
of war and natural disasters. Others have lost investments and had
bank accounts dwindle with reduced interest rates or unexpected
expenses. Some national borders and the configurations of many
nations are radically different than they were a year ago. What does
abide? What sustains us? Why do we go on? Are we like those of
whom Cervantes speaks, who see life only as it is and not as it ought
to be? Where do we turn to shape a sustaining vision of the present
and future?

The Apostle Paul offers an important clue in the familiar words,
"And now faith, hope, and love abide, these three; and the greatest of
these is love" (1 Corinthians 13:13). This sounds sensible enough.
And, to be sure, Christians say that theirs is the religion of love! Yet
Christians themselves, the church and Christian organizations, have
often reversed Paul's order and in reality have made this verse read,
"And now faith, hope, and love abide; and the greatest of these is
faith."

The early church councils placed strong emphasis on correct
statements of belief which eliminated heresies—hence, the rise of
various creedal statements and catechisms. Church history is filled
with heresy trials. Though numerous persons were tried for believing
"wrong" things and doing "wrong" things, no one was ever tried for
loving too little or too much. The Spanish Inquisition and the
Crusades emphasized what is "right" and who is right, but hardly
how to love, especially the unloved.

No religion on this globe is more fragmented and divided than Christianity, and yet those who follow Jesus claim that love reigns in their lives. There is enough that divides us to make us want to be called by different names: Orthodox, Roman Catholic, Baptist, Presbyterian, Lutheran, Methodist, Nazarene, etc. All these names immediately evoke ideas about belief but not necessarily about love! Yet, Paul says, the greatest of faith, hope, and love is love!

To what then will our lives bear witness in the present, for a lifetime, for eternity? Hopefully, to Paul's vision—the greatest is love! It is love that draws us to one another and to God. It is love that gives faith its meaning. Love that empties itself for others, God, and all creation is resistless! This is what we must see ever before us in thought, word, and deed as seminal to our daily witness.

What do we learn about this view of life from the Scriptures?

Resistless love witnesses to God as love, or in John's words, to the reality—God is love.

Jesus asks us as he asked his own disciples: "Have you been so long with me and having eyes do you not see and having ears do you not hear?" Have you no clear vision?

The vision of divine love is as ancient as God's creation. God creates out of love. Here are other glimpses of the love vision from scripture. In remembering God's deliverance from Egyptian bondage, the Song of Moses celebrates the vision: "In your steadfast love you led the people whom you redeemed" (Exodus 15:13). The priests of Israel affirm the love that one personifies or acts out in daily living: "You shall love your neighbor as you love yourself" (Leviticus 19:18). Deuteronomy 6:5 describes the response to such love: "You shall love the Lord your God with all your heart, and with all your soul, and with all your might." And we are admonished to recite these words, to teach them to our children, and to put them on the doorposts of our houses and on our gates. Note what else it says in Deuteronomy: "You shall also love the stranger, for you were strangers in Egypt" (Deuteronomy 10:19). The psalmist affirms the heart of the love vision and what abides in exclaiming: "For God's steadfast love endures forever" (136:1). Those who see the vision of love are called to "hold fast to love and justice" (Hosea 12:6). And the prophet Zechariah adjures us: "love truth and peace" (Zechariah 8:19).

All of the passages just quoted are from the Hebrew Scriptures. This is the testimony of love expressed for the world of ancient Israel. But what did God's people do with this vision? They turned it not into a love reality for all human beings but rather into a nightmare of madness and enmity. Yes, there are moments when we get a glimpse of the vision become reality in a Joseph or a Jonathan, but on the whole spiritual and social turmoil, societal strife, war, and political and religious divisiveness among God's people give the love vision little chance of fulfillment.

Resistless love witnesses to Jesus as the fullest expression of God's love.

The love of Jesus has a special quality about it. It is God's love on our behalf. "As the father has loved me, so have I loved you" (John 15:9). This is the Christ of whom Paul writes that he "loved me and gave himself for me" (Galatians 2:20). The self-giving quality of Jesus' love becomes the reason for our love: "We love because he first loved us" (1 John 4:19).

The love of Jesus exemplifies and embodies a love that empties itself for others at all costs, even death upon a cross.

We learn as children:

Jesus loves me, this I know
for the Bible tells me so;
little ones to him belong,
they are weak but he is strong.

Yes, Jesus loves me.
Yes, Jesus loves me,
Yes, Jesus loves me,
The Bible tells me so.[2]

There is no greater truth that we can learn than this—that we are loved by Jesus, who is the ultimate expression of love.

But how do we know this love? We know it by becoming ourselves expressions of the same kind of self-giving love. This is not easy. It means we must love the unlovely, such as Cyrano de Bergerac[3] with his elongated nose or an elephant man. It is much more than that, however—it is daring to make friends of the unlovely as Jesus did. It is daring to invite them into our homes, to our tables, and into our lives.

To see Jesus as the fullest expression of God's love means that as we follow him, we follow his example of love. We personify his self-giving love. We give ourselves in love even for the most unlikely, especially the poor.

> The poor as Jesus' bosom-friends,
>   the poor he makes his latest care,
> to all his followers commends,
>   and wills us on our hands to bear;
> the poor our dearest care we make,
> and love them for our Savior's sake.[4]

We are told in scripture that "perfect love casts out fear" (1 John 4:18). Many prefer, however, to live by the proverb: "Birds of a feather flock together." But when Jesus' love fully overtakes our being, we are no longer afraid to give and give again of ourselves to the lost, the least, and the last.

Here's a way described by the eighteenth century poet-priest, Charles Wesley, to begin each day with the love vision.

> Away with our fears!
> The Godhead appears
> In Christ reconciled,
> The Father of mercies in Jesus the Child.

> He comes from above,
> In manifest Love,
> The desire of our eyes,
> The meek Lamb of God, in a manger he lies.

> Made flesh for our sake,
> That we might partake
> The Nature Divine,
> And again in his image, his holiness shine.

Then let us believe,
And gladly receive
The Tidings they bring,
Who publish to Sinners their Savior and King.

And while we are here,
Our King shall appear,
His Spirit impart,
And form his full image of Love in our heart.[5]

And form his full image of Love in our heart! Here is a primary key to the witness of resistless love. The full image of God's love, the Savior Jesus Christ, is formed in our hearts.

Resistless love witnesses to ourselves as love.

It is one thing to see God as love and Jesus as the fullest expression of God's love, but to see yourself as love—one literally filled with God's love–is to live the reality that God is love. Others can encounter God's love through you. This is why there is such wisdom in the words of Leviticus 19 that are quoted in the New Testament (Mark 12:31): "Love your neighbor as you love yourself." If we do not love ourselves, we cannot love others. We must say constantly to ourselves, "I am love."

Yet, we tend to distort the love, if we may believe the Scriptures and human history. Are not the words of the Scriptures verified in our own world? "You love evil more than good" (Psalm 52:3). "You love all words that devour" (Psalm 52:4). Are we like the Pharisees who "neglect justice and the love of God" (Luke 11:42)?

What are we to be like—we who see the love vision, we who personify love? Once again, the Scriptures help us focus the vision.

We are to love our enemies (Matthew 5:44).
Love does no wrong to a neighbor (Romans 13:10).
Knowledge puffs up, but love builds up (1 Corinthians 8:1).
We are to make love our aim (1 Corinthians 14:1).
All that we do should be done in love (1 Corinthians 16:14).
Greet one another with a kiss of love (1 Peter 5:14).
Have love for one another (John 15:35).

The Scriptures offer us also words of caution regarding the witness of love.

> Do not "love in word or speech but in truth and action"
>   (1 John 3:18).
> Do not love the world or things (1 John 2:5).
> Those who do not love, do not know God (1 John 4:8).
> "Those who say, 'I love God,' and hate their brothers and sisters,
> are liars; for those who do not love a brother or sister whom they
> have seen, cannot love God whom they have not seen"
>   (1 John 4:20).

Love is the common denominator of life. It is the determinant of existence. It is the redeemer of all that is evil in this world. As we personify it, as we empty ourselves in love for God and love for others, they too can come to know, experience, and share love with others. What shall we bequeath our children, friends, enemies? Will our legacy be the witness of love in our daily lives?

In Tennessee Williams' play *Cat on a Hot Tin Roof,* the patriarch of a wealthy estate is terminally ill and his children are greedily awaiting the distribution of his fortune at his death. The son whom he perhaps loves the most is an alcoholic and cares nothing about all this wealth. His marriage is in shambles and he has little reason for living. The old man finds himself on one occasion in the basement of his mansion, which is filled with luxurious items that he and his wife brought back from their world travels and that they have no room for in their expansive and lavish house. His son appears and begins ranting and raving about senseless luxury, and as things are thrown about, suddenly the old man comes upon an old hat. He becomes pensive and begins to tell his son the hat belonged to his father, a man who never amounted to anything—he was just a hobo. After a night around a fire in the woods, his father died. He dug a grave for him, buried him, and swore that he would not wind up like his father, who left him nothing. Then he paused—there was total silence—and he said that he did leave him something: he left him love.

God has left us self-giving, selfless, enduring, healing, resistless love in his son Jesus Christ who comes with the words, "A new commandment I give to you that you love one another as I have loved you."

According to the Apostle Paul, when the full image of Christ's love is formed in our hearts, we will be patient and kind, not envious, boastful, arrogant, or rude. We will not insist on our own way. We will not be irritable or resentful. We will not rejoice in wrongdoing, but will rejoice in the truth. We will be able to bear whatever comes. We will be able to believe, hope, and endure all. If we are not like that, the full image of Christ's love has not been formed in our hearts. It does not matter how much we know, or how strong we think our faith is — we are nothing. We can be the most generous giver in our congregation or community, but our generosity amounts to nothing unless the image of Christ's love is formed in our hearts.

Is this the testimony of our lives? Without love as the vantage point from which we view and live our lives, it is impossible for the *audible* word to become the *visible* word. The daily witness of resistless love enables the articulation of the Good News with our lives. "St. John Chrysostom insisted that church members' mutual love was the only effective missionary method."[6]

"You will know them by their fruits," (Matthew 7:20) says Jesus. When we love, others will come to know love. This is the heart of witnessing through resistless love. When we witness with love, it will be resistless.

In the next chapters we shall turn to some images used in the Bible that are foundational for such witnessing today.

4. The Witness of Evangelizing Love

Evangelism is understood in a variety of ways throughout the Christian churches of the world. Many see it simply as telling the Good News to those who have not heard it. Some unequivocally verbalize it as "leading others to Christ." If you evangelize, you tell the story and in so doing bring others to salvation. Many would prefer a much broader definition of evangelism which places more emphasis on the impact of the story than on the telling of the story itself. They raise a question about what difference it makes if you tell the story, even "lead someone to Christ," if you express no ongoing concern for the redemptive work of Christ in that person's whole life and environment. Who bears the responsibility for the consequences of evangelizing? Still others place a strong emphasis on the claim God makes upon us through Jesus Christ, rather than the claim we make upon him and hence upon salvation.

There are already hundreds, if not thousands, of books dealing with the subject of evangelism's definitions, strategies, methodologies. Many have slogans and bywords, or specific styles, which may or may not be effective for either mass or personal evangelism. They may not address the uniqueness of various cultures, diverse settings (e.g., urban, rural, multiethnic), or the religious, political, and economic conditions that determine successful approaches to evangelism. This is to say nothing of the methods of imposition whereby hoards of people across centuries were forced by monarchs and church leaders to be baptized in the name of winning souls to Christ and expanding the Kingdom of God. For example, Charlemagne drove the Saxons through the Elba River, declaring them baptized, and King Ferdinand and Queen Isabella sought new converts for Roman Catholicism in the New World through Columbus.

This is not the place to rehearse evangelistic methods and the plethora of strategies set in motion across the centuries by the Christian church and organizations or individuals claiming to be Christian. It is, however, the place to raise anew the question of what the ultimate goal of evangelizing should be. The answer for many is crystal clear—"the saving of souls." Others would respond different-ly and maintain that God calls the church to be an ongoing caring/redemptive community proclaiming the Good News of salva-tion in every aspect of its life. In other words, God summons indi-viduals to transformation *in* the world, as well as the transformation *of* a world where transformed and untransformed persons live in har-mony and discord. "The saving of souls" then is personal *and* social. Such transformation has varied dimensions, for the quality of indi-vidual and corporate life is determined by the depth of the transfor-mation. One thing is certain from the Holy Scriptures: *Jesus Christ changes lives and changes life, and the context of transformation is the church, the body of Christ.* The biblical summons to transforma-tion is not merely individual but corporate. Christ does not just make new creations of us; he makes "*all things* new." Furthermore, his is not solely a summons to human beings at the expense of the rest of creation, but to the reclaiming and renewing of creation. It is not enough to save a soul if the earth is raped. According to the Hebrew and Greek Scriptures, saving the earth is part of God's redemptive and renewing process (see Psalm 104, especially verse 30).

Too often in the history of the church's outreach, it has opted for cheap evangelistic propaganda in a singular quest for the personal transformation of individuals. Or it has actively sought transforma-tion of society and environment at the expense of concern about the changed lives of individuals. Frequently, those who have sought *per-sonal* transformation have neglected *societal* transformation and those who have sought the latter have neglected the former. And often those emphasizing one or the other have spoken different lan-guages. Of course, in recent years there have been many "evangeli-cals" who have developed a penetratingly effective and socially engaging ministry and message. They have become deeply con-cerned about personal transformation that has social impact and about the renewal of *all* creation in and through Christ. There have also been "turnarounds" by some who previously had neglected the arena of personal transformation and dedicated themselves solely to social action. Sometimes the criticism is harsh between those who want personal transformation above all else and those who stress the social aspects of redemption. The myths circulated by their followers do more to destroy the effectiveness of Christian witness than to bring Christ's healing to a broken world. Interestingly Christians with radically differing views on evangelism often sing the same songs/hymns and pray the same prayers. In practice, however, they intentionally do not attend the same church or support the same projects.

How is one to reconcile a broken and fragmented church with a unifying and holistic gospel message of love for all people? The face of the Christian church is no flawless example of God's holistic, unifying love. The church is filled with those who are absolutely certain that they have a superior right to the gospel message and its proclamation. They are sure that their own particular theological bias is *the* key to the salvation of the world. And the cry goes up anew to a church which after twenty centuries is still in search of unity and concord:

> Ye different sects who all declare:
> Lo, here is Christ or Christ is there!
> Your stronger proofs divinely give,
> And show me where the Christians live!
> (Charles Wesley)

"Ah," many say, "you don't need the church! That is the great historical blunder of Christianity. Being Christian is not about being in the *church*. It is about being in *Christ*. The church is merely an institution structured by human beings." This argument simply ignores both the language and history of the New Testament, as though both do not exist. It is much too easy to substitute western individualism for the concept of "the body of Christ," which was born in the Near East. It is much easier to think individually than corporately. It is much easier to ignore culture and ideas foreign to one's own. One cannot read the four gospels and the Book of Acts, however, and aver that the church as an idea and as an *organized* community of the faithful is completely foreign to Jesus and St. Paul. One's theology of the church determines one's view of evangelism. Is it something practiced by the church, the individual, or both? Does the individual need "the body of Christ" in order to engage in evangelism? Is evangelism the lifestyle of the "body of Christ"? Is it an individual or corporate responsibility?

Where do we begin with a theology of "resistless love," love that evangelizes because of what it is and does, rather than what it says? The summons to a transformed life with God is central to the biblical message. The Hebrew Scriptures beckon to a transformed life. Hence, we begin where they begin—with creation.

A Theology of Creation

Is the purpose of creation according to the Book of Genesis primarily the "salvation of souls"? That is certainly difficult to maintain on the basis of the biblical account. There are many theories about the "why" of creation, but none seems completely satisfying, for we do not discover specifically why God began the creation process. It has been maintained by some that human beings are created out of the desire for fellowship, and James Weldon Johnson's *God's Trombones* is perhaps one of the most eloquent folk expressions of this view. But why create the earth? Does nothingness (formlessness and void) require "something" to fill the void or is that a flaw in human logic? Why create human beings? Is God so alone?

The "why" of creation is an eternal enigma. This nagging question is at the heart of the human dilemma, for it raises the question whether life has any meaning at all! What else is there besides mere existence and death? And why did this strange cycle begin? One response of theology is that God created human beings in the divine image with specific purposes and restraints. Humans breached that relationship through rebellion, and thus began the estrangement of human beings from God. Adam and Eve were instructed by God not to eat of the tree of knowledge of good and evil. Nevertheless, they did precisely what they were told not to do. This story becomes the bulwark of numerous theologies of evangelism, for it is the *fallen-ness* of human beings embodied in Adam and Eve which is what "telling the Good News" seeks to transform into wholeness. It seeks to turn estrangement and alienation into reclaimed relationship and salvation.

The Genesis story indicates that God's creation begins with boundaries and that human relationship to God has its own boundaries. Whatever one makes of the boundaries themselves, it seems clear from the Genesis creation story that at least part of the meaning of why there is creation at all has to do with relationship—between the Creator and the creation. But this relationship has been so diversely interpreted, especially in the arena of evangelism, that one often wonders when one reads various theologians whether they are reading the same biblical text. Unfortunately, much of human creation's energy is expended in living "beyond" the boundaries of creation and in struggling to mend the boundaries once they are broken.

The Genesis creation story may not be specifically about the "salvation of souls," but it definitely describes the broken relationship between those who are divinely created and God the Creator. The remainder of the Scriptures then addresses the brokenness of this relationship and its restoration to the wholeness of creation's beginning.

The scriptural view of creation is holistic. Even though human beings have responsibility as stewards of creation, the Scriptures do not maintain that they are above the created world to the extent that they may misuse it. Nevertheless, it is a human tendency to categorize all aspects of creation and to conclude that certain facets of it are expendable. For example, some aver that since animals cannot think, they are not as important to creation as human beings who can reason and consult intelligently with one another. Others may claim that trees are inanimate objects without the faculties of human emotion and intelligence and, hence, are not as important as humans. Such positions are modes of thought that have brought the world a plethora of ecological imbalances. The Genesis story supports the conclusion that God does care about all parts of creation, such as rainforests and rivers. Creation is God's handiwork. It is declared "good" by God, and human beings are charged with a just stewardship of that creation.

The Genesis creation story, however, also has a clearly defined view of human beings: they are corrupt (Genesis 6:11–12). Though declared "good," like the whole of creation, they have turned to their own way. And the rest of the biblical account addresses the corruption which results in the estrangement of human beings from one another, from the earth, and from God. Human history is a rehearsal of this estrangement of the created from creation and, hence, from the Creator.

There is a tendency, however, to interpret the creation story as part of a graceless Old Testament world in which "fallen" mortals are enmeshed in sin through the law, which cannot be a means of God's grace. But this is a misreading of the intention in the Scriptures and of the Scriptures themselves. One must read this story holistically, too. It does seem that the human situation is hopeless, as Adam and Eve are flagrantly disobedient to God and are destined to die for their action. Yet, they do not die—*grace revealed*—(though some commentators would maintain that at least spiritual death takes place), but they are cast out of the Garden of Eden and marked for a life of toil.

In the story of Cain and Abel, one encounters the senselessness and hopelessness of human violence and yet, even as Cain is expelled from the Garden of Eden, inscribed upon his forehead is a sign that God is his protector—*grace revealed.*

Surely, however, the tower of Babel story brings humankind to the reality of the hopelessness of fraternization, socialization, and human communication. Although all inhabitants of the earth and all creation groan in despair at the failure of being able to live and speak with one another, at the moment when it seems all is lost, God makes a new covenant with Abraham, the man of faith who goes out not knowing where he is going, that in and through him all the nations of the earth shall be blessed. Out of chaos God renews the covenant and gives a blessing—*grace revealed.*

Creation, according to the Scriptures, is revealed and active grace. Charles Wesley aptly bids the community of faith remember that God's grace is not stagnant or stymied by inertia. It is energizing, a grace which creates—that is, calls into being and existence.

> O God of our life, we hallow thy name;
> Our business and strife is thee to proclaim.
> Accept our thanksgiving for *creating grace*;
> The living, the living shall show forth thy praise.[1]

Without a holistic theology of creation, one is in grave danger of accepting a theology of evangelism that may stress the salvation of human beings at the expense of the rest of creation. Do the Scriptures say that you may rape and abuse God's creation at all costs for the sake of saving one soul? The New Testament story of the ninety and nine indicates that God does care intensely about the redemption of *every* individual, just as the caring shepherd goes in search of a single sheep gone astray. However, the Scriptures also maintain that all creation groans for the salvation of God (see Romans 8:22–25). The psalmist declares:

> O Lord, how manifold are your works!
> *In wisdom you have made them all;*
> the earth is full of your creatures....
>
> *When you send forth your Spirit,*
> *they are created;*
> *and you renew the face of the ground.*
> (Psalm 104:24, 30, KJV)

Charles Wesley responds to the psalmist's claim with this holistic view of creation:

> Author of every work divine,
> Who dost through both creations shine,
>   The God of nature and of grace!
> Thy glorious steps in all we see,
> And wisdom attribute to thee,
>   And power, and majesty, and praise.
>
> Thou dost create the earth anew,
> (Its Maker and Preserver too,)
>   By thine almighty arm sustain:
> Nature perceives thy secret force,
> And stills holds on her even course
>   And owns thy providential reign.
>
> Thou art the Universal Soul,
> The Plastic[2] power that fills the whole,
>   And governs earth, air, sea, and sky:
> The creatures all thy breath receive,
> And who, by thy inspiring, live,
>   Without thy inspiration, die.[3]

A theology of evangelization grounded in the whole of the Scriptures and faith in a God who fills the whole of creation with life-giving Spirit, must call for the redemption of all creation. The human response to the call to salvation is decisive in the redemptive process. In a world where plant and animal life, seas, rivers, and rainforests are threatened with destruction precipitated by the *genius* or *insanity* of technology, it is easy to perceive that human decision has brought God's creation under attack. The plethora of new diseases unleashed by technological *advances* and *regressions* are constant reminders of the brevity of human life. One need only think of the host of diseases precipitated among human beings by the advent of processed sugar. Creation, God's creating grace, is afflicted with pain and even death through human *ingenuity* and *apathy!* Yet, Charles Wesley poignantly avers, "Thou dost create the world anew"!

New Creation in Christ

A theology of evangelization for our time must plead for the *new creation* of God's creatures in the redemptive love of Christ. But that is not enough, for God shines "through both creations": the world of nature *and* humankind, according to Psalm 104 and Wesley's paraphrase. God's wisdom, power, and majesty are not limited merely to mortals but pervade *all* creation. Is it possible the psalmist is right—that God not only makes persons new but makes the earth new as well? Charles Wesley does not perceive the psalmist's comments as belonging merely to the future creation of a new earth. No, God's creative process is a present reality, for

> Nature perceives thy secret force,
> And still holds on her even course.

Nature harbors a divine wisdom which inaugurates seasons in most parts of the world, initiates the hibernation and migration cycles of animals, and precipitates the return of salmon to their spawning beds. There is a secret force which nature indeed perceives—a divine wisdom. As powerful as this secret force of divine wisdom is, its rhythm can be interrupted, even destroyed through the exploitation and misuse of natural resources. If we would espouse a holistic theology of creation as foundational for a theology of evangelization, we must heed Wesley's bidding to acknowledge God's "providential reign" and the Spirit of God at work as a "secret force" throughout all creation.

Wesley stresses with the psalmist that *all* creatures receive God's breath. All creation has life from God. Plants and animals receive God's *nephesh* and are alive. Some English Bible translations have misleadingly translated this Hebrew word in Genesis 2:7 as "soul," but *nephesh* is the "life principle" which distinguishes the living from the dead. According to the Scriptures, in God's creation plants, as well as animals, have *nephesh*. Both have God-given life.

Interestingly, nature (all of it, even plants and animals) somehow perceives the divine "secret force" in creation and submits to its cycle of renewal. Human beings, however, often devise means of exerting their own force against the secret force of God. Nature has been created not to satisfy human whims but for God's glory and the sustenance of creation. Nonetheless, over the centuries men and women have exploited nature for their own advantage, forgetting that the whole of creation is permeated with the creative Spirit of God. Furthermore, the Christian religious community has placed a premium on human redemption and often has not heard the rest of creation groan and wail for salvation and renewal. A theology of evangelization which emphasizes one at the expense of the other cannot be true to the Scriptures.

According to the Genesis story of creation, God's created order becomes *deformed* by the disobedience of Adam and Eve. The remainder of the Bible is the story of how the deformed or broken relationship with God *and* creation can be transformed into a healed, whole relationship, as at the birth of creation. How can human beings live in harmony with God and creation? Each implies the other—living in harmony with God means living in harmony with creation and vice versa. People were not created to live alienated from God or from creation, but to live in unity with them. The prophet Isaiah understood this well when he recorded that God, "who formed the earth and made it . . . did not create it a chaos," rather "formed it to be inhabited!" (45:18) Furthermore, Isaiah declares that God did not say to the offspring of Jacob, "Seek me in chaos" (45:19).

Nevertheless, it is clear that we live in a chaotic world because we live contrary to God's intent for the earth. It was not created for destruction but to be inhabited. The origin of such chaos is the same kind of disobedience exhibited by Adam and Eve. We satisfy our own appetites at all costs, even the rape of creation for personal and/or corporate gain. All are in desperate need of transformation to change a world which has an insatiable appetite to eat from the "tree of life" until there is no more fruit. The catalyst of this transformation and different behavior is love.

This is why a theology of creation is the vital basis of redemptive evangelizing love, for it must be holistic and not selective. Orlando Costas is right to remind us that "evangelization is a witness that takes place in a given social and historical context."[4] Before we can fully appreciate ethnic and cultural uniqueness, however, we must understand in the biblical view that the larger "context" is God's creation. This is precisely why evangelization cannot be personal *or* social. To be sure, the transformation of human hearts and minds is the beginning of creation transformation, but it is not a cure-all that absolves the transformed from engagement in the lifelong process of being instruments of God's Spirit. One cares about the transformation of human beings, *indeed,* but also about the renewal and transformation of all God's creation.

What is to be said then of the "Great Commission" of Jesus: "Go into all the world and make disciples of all nations, baptizing them in the name of the Father, the Son, and the Holy Spirit"? One may not read his words in isolation, as though he were not a person of the Hebrew Scriptures. The New Testament provides the picture of Jesus reading in the synagogue from the Isaiah scroll, and the extent to which he quotes from the Hebrew Scriptures indicates the depths to which, as a young man, he had increased in "wisdom and in years, and in divine and human favor" (Luke 2:52). He seems to have been educated in the Hebrew Scriptures as part of a strong rabbinical tradition. Could one who knew the Psalms and prophets so well simply have sought to nullify the word which he himself personified? Could it be that he was saying in the Great Commission: God is now concerned *only* with the salvation of human beings; therefore, everything else in God's creation is expendable for the salvation of souls? If that is the case, he expresses a blatant disregard for divine creation. We read in the first chapter of John, however, that the word, the *logos* personified in Jesus, was in the beginning and that through God's word all things were made. This means that Jesus is intimately bound to the whole of creation. The giving of himself is not merely to reclaim part but all of creation. The word which was in the beginning and through which all things were made becomes the force through which all things are made new.

When one speaks of resistless love today, it is clear that one is referring in particular to contextual evangelization, which takes into account the whole of one's life in the totality of one's surroundings with regard for the unique contributions that ethnicity and culture make to the fullness of Christ's witness. But this witness is never exclusively personal *or* social; it is personal *and* social! If one has had no personal encounter with Jesus Christ and has not experienced the transformation of love, one cannot participate in the social dimension of evangelization. Here one comes to a decisive point in a theology of creation, at least from a perspective which is rooted in both the Hebrew and Greek Scriptures. A holistic theology of creation as the foundation for a theology of evangelizing love mandates transformation of God's creation. The messianic hope of the Hebrew Scriptures anticipates transformation—the formation of a new people and a new earth. From the standpoint of the New Testament, it is very clear that it is precisely this kind of holistic transformation Jesus Christ inaugurates. *Jesus Christ transforms lives and transforms life; therefore, changed lives and changed life are mutual imperatives. The renewal of God's creation assumes not only the transformation of individuals but of community and environment! Gospel transformation mandates gospel community! Evangelization is about changed lives and changed life!* The lives and ministries of John and Charles Wesley were a personification of this reality. They understood the powerful mandate of God and the Scriptures that personal and social holiness be mutual imperatives.

Evangelization that focuses on the individual alone and disregards the renewal of God's whole creation may be well-meaning but it cannot be faithful to the Scriptures. Yet one asks, Is not Jesus' ministry "people-oriented"? Is he not concerned with the transformation of individuals on page after page of the New Testament? His stories are about the need for people to turn to God, change the perspectives

and ways of their lives, and become servants of God in full commitment to God and others. In the enthusiasm to read biblical stories
with an eye toward personal transformation, there is a tendency to
miss the fact that Jesus acknowledges the created order as implicit in
God's concern for creation. "Foxes have holes, and the birds of the
air have nests; but the Son of Man has nowhere to lay his head"
(Matthew 8:20). Nature has an order that functions better than the
realm of human nature, which learns and practices discrimination,
exclusion, and even creates homelessness. It is this prejudicial bent
of human nature that can also destroy the habitats of foxes and the
nesting places of birds and give people no place to lay their heads.
Further, Jesus says, "Look at the birds of the air; for they neither sow
nor reap nor gather into barns, and yet your heavenly Father feeds
them" (Matthew 6:26). Or again, "Consider the lilies of the field,
how they grow; they neither toil nor spin, yet I say to you that even
Solomon in all his glory was not clothed like one of these" (Matthew
6:28–29). Even the beauty of creation held in such regard by Jesus
can be obliterated by human waste and devastation to the extent that
such a metaphor could become meaningless. All the glory of King
Solomon's wealth and imposing reign cannot compare to the simple
beauty of a field lily! Jesus could not have anticipated an industrial-
ized world would lay waste vast areas of land that could never again
grow a lily, and to assume that he would consent to this misuse and
devastation of divine creation is a grossly misdirected reading of the
Scriptures. He would say to people of every age that one must go in
quest of the redemption of every human being at all costs—including the ultimate cost, even death upon a cross—but not with disregard for God's will for *all* creation: that it be renewed by the Spirit.

If we would live out God's mandate to bring harmony once again
to all creation through the redemptive love revealed through Jesus
Christ, how shall we evangelize this earth and those throughout it, if
not through the love which does the redeeming? If we do not love,
however, love will not evangelize. It is essential then that our view,
our vision, of this love be very clear.

"What God most cares about," says Walter Bruggemann, "is love
of God and love of neighbor,"[5] and he makes clear elsewhere in his
book *Biblical Perspectives on Evangelism* that this love includes all
creation.[6]

5. The Witness of Holy Communion

Meals are at the center of family and communal life and they play a significant role in the life of many religions. Feast days with special significance for relationships among peoples and to creation dot the annual calendar of religions of the world. Sustenance for the body is related to sustenance of the soul, the spirit, the total person. The Passover meal that Jesus celebrated with his disciples prior to his betrayal and cruciform was transformed into a sacrament through the acts of breaking bread and drinking wine, which Jesus adjured his disciples to do "in remembrance of me." Hence, the partaking of Christ's body and blood in this meal becomes the very matrix of Christian community. At this table of Christ's presence and remembrance is where the church becomes what it really is—the universal body of Christ, sealed in unity by the Holy Spirit. At this table, love of God and love of neighbor receive their fullest expression. Here one experiences God's resistless love!

Jesus' mandate to the community of faith to "do this in remembrance of me" places the table of our Lord at the center of community, spirituality, and mission. Indeed Holy Communion is for the church of Jesus Christ its point of departure for mission and evangelization and is itself a missionary event. How the church is formed as one body in this act is a mystery and the members of the body come together time and again realizing that this mystery is the true identity of the people of God. But how can this be? How can this meal be a missionary event? How can it be an evangelical meal?

Holy Communion is a meal of proclamation. It is a meal which witnesses to the reality that Christ has come and Christ will come again. St. Paul declares, "For as often as you eat this bread and drink the cup, you *proclaim* the Lord's death until he comes" (1 Corinthians 11:26). Therefore, as strange as it may sound to those who would affirm that proclamation can only be a verbal act, the apostle Paul says something quite different. In partaking of this meal, the members of the body of Christ "*proclaim* the Lord's death."

Therefore, the meal is one in which those who partake of the body and blood of Christ declare that there is power in his death and resurrection to reclaim the world through sacrificial love, a resistless love which heals the wounds of sin. Such self-giving, self-emptying love heals all sinfulness, alienation, and enmity. When the community of faith comes to the table, this is what it proclaims. It declares the message of the Good News that is at the heart of the church's mission: it is the body, blood, and resurrection of Christ that redeem and reclaim life, and send the church forth in mission!

Holy Communion is an evangelical meal. While diverse church communions set rules and standards as to who may come to God's holy table, one must not forget the power of God's grace in and through the meal to redeem. Charles Wesley affirms this power in the following selected stanzas of the hymn "Come, Sinners, to the Gospel Feast":

> Do not begin to make excuse;
> ah! do not you his grace refuse;
> your worldly cares and pleasures leave,
> and take what Jesus hath to give.
>
> Come and partake the gospel feast,
> be saved from sin, in Jesus rest;
> O taste the goodness of our God,
> and eat his flesh and drink his blood.
>
> See him set forth before your eyes;
> behold the bleeding sacrifice;
> his offered love make haste to embrace,
> and freely now be saved by grace.[1]

Hence, the meal is a feast of redemption. The "offered love" of God in Christ reclaims and nourishes those who feed upon it. They "taste the goodness of our God" in the gospel feast and the power of Christ's death and resurrection envelops their lives so that they are filled with love that dies and rises again for others and all creation.

To refuse to come to the table, Wesley reminds us, is to reject the grace of God. Where the table is neglected by faith communities and individuals within them, God's grace is refused. No worldly cares or pleasures should divert interest from this most sacred of meals.

Holy Communion is also an eschatological meal, for the body of Christ is a community of faith moving toward its *full* unity and *completion,* toward the *eschaton.* It comes to the table in unity, as one body, but amid *incompleteness.* This is twofold: (1) It is always moving toward the moment of Christ's coming, always remembering his death in the meal "until he comes." (2) It comes to the table as one body, yet broken, since though all are welcome at the feast, many bodies claiming to be the church have often excluded one another, which was never part of Christ's intention.

Nevertheless, it is in Holy Communion that the fullness of the body of Christ truly resides. It is the beginning point and sustenance of its mission and evangelization. As a body sent forth into the world to personify the love of Christ, to proclaim the Good News of redemptive love, it experiences in this meal the empowerment to fulfill such a purpose. If this meal is neglected, or relegated to secondary importance, the mission of the church loses the primary sustaining source of community. As Petros Vassiliadis appropriately emphasizes, "The church's mission is the dynamic journey of the people of God as a whole towards the *eschaton,* with the Eucharist as the point of departure."[2]

Holy Communion witnesses to unity. If Christ intended for all humankind to be included in this meal, it behooves the church of Jesus Christ to consider carefully its relationship to those it presumes to invite to the table. It is not the church that extends the invitation to the meal, but God through the divine Son, Jesus Christ. Charles Wesley once wrote some provocative lines specifically referring to this invitation:

> Come, sinners, to the gospel feast,
> let every soul be Jesus' guest.
> Ye need not one be left behind,
> for God hath bid all humankind.[3]

At the celebration of Holy Communion, each congregation, each Christian denomination, needs to look among the participants to see who has been excluded. That is an amazing revelation in our time — namely, that institutionalized churches have decided to limit the invitation of Jesus by intentionally or inadvertently excluding those who do not "belong" to a specific faith community. What could violate more the authority of the Savior and his invitation to all! These exclusions are sometimes ecclesiological, but also sociological, economical, and even political. What signal does this send to those who are marginalized, those excluded from the table, about the mission of the church and the Good News it proclaims? If Holy Communion is only reserved for a select group, by choice, church law, or inadvertent or intentional negligence, those who administer it defy the invitation of Jesus to all to be at his table.

The *epiclesis,* the prayer for the invocation of the Holy Spirit in the Holy Communion liturgy, is foundational for the mission of the church, the body of Christ. Such a mission seeks the worldwide unity of all people of the earth in Christ, that they may be redeemed through his sacrifice and resurrection.

> Pour out your Holy Spirit on us gathered here,
> and on these gifts of bread and wine.
> Make them be for us the body and blood of Christ,
> that we may be for the world the body of Christ,
> redeemed by his blood.
> By your Spirit make us one with Christ,
> one with each other,
> and one in ministry to all the world,
> until Christ comes in final victory,
> and we feast at his heavenly banquet.
>
> Through your Son Jesus Christ,
> with the Holy Spirit in your holy church,
> all honor and glory is yours, almighty Father,
> now and forever.[4]

What more significant prayer can the community of faith pray than this one? What prayer expresses better the mission witness of the church?

> . . . make us one with Christ,
> one with each other,
> and one in ministry to all the world.

Holy Communion is the means of grace wherein the Holy Spirit through the body and blood of Jesus Christ molds anew the people of God as the body of Christ for the world, redeemed by his blood, which is the missional hope of the church for the world—that all people will be incorporated into this unity. Thus the church lives this redeemed unity as a witness to the world.

The witness of the church to the world is a broken one, because of the brokenness, the divided nature of the church, and it is in the celebration of Holy Communion, the coming in humbleness to the Lord's table, that unity must be sought, if this celebration is to have the integrity and the openness with which Christ imbued it when he extended the invitation to all.

In Holy Communion, the church proclaims a message to the world. One dimension of this proclamation has been mentioned already. It proclaims Christ's death until he comes. But another dimension of this proclamation is that the church declares its own broken nature and the ineffectiveness of Christians throughout the world to fulfill the invocation of the Holy Spirit that we be made one with Christ, with each other, and with the rest of the world.

Holy Communion is the empowering source of mission. Those who come to the table leave renewed in body, mind, and spirit. They experience what it means to die and rise with Christ and thus the wholeness of self-giving love, resistless love. When they rise to depart the table, they rise to personify anew this selfless, resistless love that heals and makes whole.

Those who come to the table rise empowered to spread the word of God in thought, word, and deed. They rise to follow in the path Christ has trod—to personify a cruciform life of self-emptying, resistless love. Through this meal, Christ imbues the community of faith with strength to witness and serve. The gifts of nature, grain from the field and fruit of the vine, transformed through the presence of Christ and love, are the empowering source of restoration and witness. Hence, the eternal song of mission to be sung by those who rise from the table is the song of life and *resistless* love uniting all sisters and brothers.

The remembrance to which we are called reminds us of those who have not received the bread and wine, those who hunger but have not been fed. Hence, the communicants are empowered to share this meal and its power with those who have no bread or drink on the table: in refugee camps with those famished in body and spirit, in hospitals, prisons, orphanages, welfare homes, and city streets where human spirits hunger for freedom, love, and new life. Christians partaking of the meal experience that Christ has given his life that they might bear the burdens and participate in the lives of all who suffer and hunger for the bread of life.

Part 2

Biblical Metaphors For Christian Witness in the New Millennium

6. Mustard Seed
Preparing for Witness: Matthew 13

In the 13th chapter of Matthew's Gospel, Jesus describes the kingdom of heaven as a mustard seed that someone took and sowed in his field. It is the smallest of all seeds, but when it has grown it is the greatest of shrubs," and the scriptural passage suggests that "the birds of the air come and make nests in its branches" (13:31–32). On a number of occasions Jesus uses the image of the seed and sower to explain the believer's faithful activity in living. This is nothing new, for the Old Testament prophets Jeremiah and Micah also speak of sowing and reaping.

Preparation and Planting

Without focusing too much on the mustard seed itself and the phenomenon of a tiny seed that produces large results, consider first that the planting of the seed that is the initial and decisive act which leads to growth. Planting requires no words, no lengthy discussion, but rather tilling and preparing the soil and sowing the seed.

My father loved to plant a vegetable garden and watch the plants grow. I remember my excitement as a little boy when I was allowed to walk up and down the furrows of plowed ground and place the seed in the soil for a small crop of corn. Day after day when I finished my chores, I would hurry over to the field to see whether the corn had begun to emerge from the ground. Days passed, rains came, and it seemed an eternity, for nothing was sprouting from the ground. Then one morning before my father left for his office, he called me and said, "Son, the corn's up!" I raced out of the house and over to the field to confirm what he said. He was right. The corn was up! What a thrill I had, as I viewed the first blades of green peeking out of the brown earth.

From that point onward the growth of the corn seemed to me like magic. The green blades of the corn grew longer, then came the stalks, which became taller and taller. Finally, tiny ears of corn began to appear. I simply could not believe that all this came from the tiny seeds I had placed in the ground.

Then the wonders increased, for my father had planted squash, tomatoes, butter beans, field peas, string beans, and even a little patch of dill. I wondered how all of these different plants could have come from tiny seeds. They were all so different in shape and color.

I learned very quickly the value of preparation for planting, for if no one prepares the soil and plants the seed, nothing grows. While my father was not a farmer by profession, he knew the art of gardening and the important principles vital to a thriving vegetable garden: turn the soil well before planting, use appropriate natural fertilizer, plant the seed in season, provide adequate water, and keep out the weeds.

Sowing the Good News of the gospel of Jesus Christ is analogous to the planting process I learned from my father. We must sow the seeds of God's resistless love or else love will not grow. But there must be proper preparation of the garden and care of the soil. You cannot withhold water, neglect the weeds, and expect a fruitful garden.

To be a mustard seed evangel is the vocation of all followers of Jesus. They spend their lives sowing the seeds of love wherever they go. They do not do it randomly but with careful preparation. They prepare the soil in themselves by rooting out all weeds of sinfulness such as apathy, bad habits, waywardness, and anger that stunt the growth of love in the garden of their own lives. Only in this manner can they hope to prepare the soil of the lives around them for the sowing of God's word and a fruitful witness to Christ's resistless love.

The Seed

Everyone is a sower of seed throughout life, and the Scriptures teach us that we shall reap what we sow. Therefore, seed selection is vital to a fruitful garden. We have sometimes heard it said of others that they are "sowing their wild oats." In other words, they are living contrary to a fruitful and productive life, contrary to the way God would have them be.

What seed will we sow? A mustard seed evangel sows the seed of the gospel: joy, patience, kindness, compassion, grace, hope, love.

When parents sow the seed of loving patience in an obstinate child instead of seeds of anger and frustration, there is an opportunity for such seed to take root in the soil of the child's own heart and soul so that he/she may grow into a loving and patient adult. It is difficult for a child to become that which the parents have not exemplified or modeled.

The planter or sower, however, must be very careful about the selection of the seed. Just any seed will not do. You must know what you want. You cannot plant the seed of a briar bush and expect to get violets. This is a principle that is vital to followers of Jesus Christ, and especially to their witnessing in daily life. Sow the seed of anger and reap hatred; sow the seed of love and reap peace. Sow the seed of despair and reap depression; sow the seed of confidence and reap hope.

When you hold a small seed, like a mustard seed, in your hand and gaze at it, think of the potential in the small round mass. It is difficult to imagine that with proper nourishment it could one day be a large plant or shrub. But this is the miracle of nature and nurture in God's creation—the smallest of seeds can produce amazing results.

This is equally true of our inward and outward spiritual growth. Such growth is directly related to that which we sow in our own hearts and souls and the mental, physical, and spiritual nurture to which we commit ourselves in daily living. If we put Christ at the center of our thinking, physical development, and inner reflection, we can expect to assume his demeanor of caring, healing, and redeeming love. Slowly the seed of self-giving, resistless love sown in his ministry, on the cross of Calvary, and in his resurrection takes root and begins to grow.

If we sow the seed of Christ's love wherever we are and among those with whom we find ourselves, we may or may not see immediate results, but where the seeds of Christ's love take root in the hearts of women, men, youth, and children, the fruits of love will grow and the results of their growth will be amazing. God's word is the redemptive word of love for all people, and that word does not return to God empty. Like the mustard seed, when sown, it produces amazing results.

At the turn of the century in the Baltic state of Lithuania, a small group of Lutherans who had been ridiculed by fellow Christians for their anti-alcohol views, their desire for lives shaped by intensive Bible study, and a deep yearning for holiness, organized a small congregation in the city of Kaunas. In 1901, after contact with a Methodist pastor from Königsberg, Germany, the congregation was officially recognized as the first Methodist Episcopal congregation on the soil of the old Russian empire.

Everywhere the members of this congregation and its pastor (first assigned in 1905) went, they sowed the seeds of the gospel of Christ's love. Like the mustard seed, the work of this small band of believers began to grow. Within a few years there were six primary congregations and a number of smaller ones throughout Lithuania.

In 1909 the first chapel was built in Kybartai, and two years later a beautiful church building was dedicated in the city of Kaunas. During the years of Lithuanian independence, 1919–1939, the Methodist Episcopal Church flourished and grew throughout the country. The sown seeds were bearing fruit.

Then came World War II, and the country was ravaged first by the Russians, a second time by the Germans, and yet a third time with the final Soviet takeover of Lithuania in 1944. At the last worship service of The Methodist Church[1] of Kaunas in June of 1944, before the communists closed the church's doors and confiscated the building, the congregation sang as one of the last songs of worship:

> The cause is yours, Lord Jesus Christ,
>   the cause on which we stand;
> Trusting in you we shall persist,
>   for all is in your hand.[2]

They were confident that the cause of Jesus Christ, the gospel sown in love, could not be obliterated and one day would bloom again. Its roots were so deep that it would hold fast and emerge once more.

Year in, year out, the old church stood in Kaunas as a silent sentinel to the gospel, a monument to nonverbal evangelism. Where no gospel could be uttered, it continued to proclaim without a word to all who passed by: "There was once a band of people who built this tower and these walls with loving hands to embrace others with Christ's love." Even when the Soviets made the church into a warehouse, a dance hall, a movie theater, and finally a sports club for children and youth, the stones proclaimed in their silence, "God loves you!"

Over fifty years passed until one day God sent this author and his colleague, W. James White, along with a former Lithuanian Methodist youth pastor, Arthur Leifert, who had not been home for fifty-five years because of the war, to that old church, where miraculously someone opened the doors for us. After a small band of the former members was found, the congregation was reorganized two years later.

The first act of the little band of surviving members, the first time they were allowed to reenter the church building, was to raise their voices in song with the words of the hymn which still resounded in their hearts from the last worship service in the church in 1944, which they had attended as children.

For over fifty years it seemed that the seeds of the gospel of love that had been sown in that place had been fully uprooted and would never again bear fruit. But God's miracle of growth defies all forces of oppression and tyranny, and from the soil of Lithuania God raised up once again the faithful to proclaim and live the gospel of Christ's redeeming love sown so long ago.

What Do Mustard Seed Evangels Do?

(1) Mustard seed evangels prepare the soil of their own hearts and souls by sowing there the seed of the gospel of Christ's redeeming love. This soil must be fertilized with prayer, disciplined reading of the Holy Scriptures, regular worship and praise of God, attendance upon the means of God's grace, the sacraments of the church, and deeds of kindness and compassion which seek nothing in return.

(2) In like manner, mustard seed evangels sow seed with anticipation that God's miracle of growth will indeed bear the fruits of the gospel of love, among which are love, patience, kindness, reverence, forgiveness, goodness, and mercy. One may indeed expect amazing

results, even if they are not immediately realizable. They may come generations later.

(3) Mustard seed evangels sow the seed of the gospel of Christ's love wherever they are. They know that sowing requires not a word; it requires the preparation of the soil, the selection of the seed, planting, and keeping out all weeds that would hinder the growth of the fruits of love.

(4) Mustard seed evangels know that, if they do not sow there will be no growth. One cannot retain the gospel of love and its fruits for oneself and expect others to be loving. Love is selfless. It gives of itself again and again for others. You cannot be a mustard seed evangel and save the seed of the gospel of love for yourself. The seeds are for sowing and growing. Mustard seed evangels are sowers!

Put these principles into practice in your life and seeds of love will take root in your life and in those about you. Every time you do a loving deed, every time you extend a loving hand, every time you embrace another with love, every time you love the unlovely and unloving, you are sowing seeds that will bear amazing fruit just like the mustard seed. Be a mustard seed evangel and you will be an enduring witness of resistless love!

7. Light
Deciding to Follow Jesus: Matthew 5:14

In the Sermon on the Mount (Matthew 5–7) Jesus makes a determinative statement for all evangels of God's love: "You are the light of the world" (5:14). It is precisely this word, this metaphor, that is applied to Jesus, who is called "the light of the world," in the Gospel of John. Those who follow the Light are bearers of the light.

During this sermon on a hill by the Sea of Galilee, Jesus may well have looked up into the mountains, seen the city of Safad nestling on the crest of the mountain, and pointed to it, saying, "A city set on a hill cannot be hid." Those who proclaim God's Good News of redemptive love in their lives are like the city on the hill. Their identity cannot be hidden. It is as obvious as the city on the hill itself. You cannot overlook the follower of Jesus who is permeated by his self-giving love. Yet, the purpose of being filled with such love is not so that one may not be overlooked. The person's demeanor is obvious and no one has to ask what is the most important thing in his or her life. That person is a personification of love and speaks loving words, does loving deeds, and thinks loving thoughts.

The Nature and Qualities of the Light

The nature and qualities of the light mentioned in the Scriptures give us guidance on what it means to embody the light and to be light for ourselves and others.

(1) The Book of Genesis affirms that the *light originates from God*. "Then God said, 'Let there be light,' and there was light" (Genesis 1:3). The light we embody, the light we emit, issues from God. This is the primary starting point from which our life in the light and with the light begins. We are not the origin of the light. God is.

(2) *Light overcomes fear.* The psalmist sings, "The Lord is my light and my salvation, whom shall I fear?" (Psalm 27:1)

(3) *Light overcomes darkness.* The light with which God illu-

mines our lives is not overcome by darkness (John 1:5). The fears and anxieties that lurk in the shadows and darkness of our lives have no place to hide once the light of Christ fills our lives, and they cannot exist in the brightness of God's love light, for it is love that casts out fear. God's evangels of redeeming and resistless love also bear the light of God's word that is a lamp to one's own feet and those of others (Psalm 119:105). When you let your light shine, others will know that the light of God's word guides your feet. This requires, however, diligent study and a lifelong commitment to be instructed by the word.

The prophet Isaiah admonished the people of Israel and us to "walk in the light of the Lord." One can walk in all kinds of light in this world: the light of the minds of others, the light of one's own mind, the light of fame and fortune, etc. Isaiah encourages everyone across the ages, however, to "walk in the light of the Lord."

In one of the Servant Songs, the prophet also announces that the Servant will be a light to the nations. As a follower of the Servant of all servants and the Light of all light, one is a light to others, for the follower emits the light of the Servant Jesus.

It is a challenging task, a challenging vocation, to be light that issues from God in the world, for that light is not overcome by darkness. It sheds the light of God's word on the path of others to guide their feet, and in the presence of that light is the place one spends one's entire life. This is a challenge indeed! But this is the evangel's calling, the calling of every follower of Jesus Christ.

Trusting in the Light

It is one thing to decide to walk in the light and quite another to trust in the light. There are innumerable stories of those at sea who have been lost in a storm and it was the beacon of a lighthouse that brought them to safety. They fixed their course on the light and, struggling to stay the course of their vessel amid raging waves and turbulent waters, they reached safety. Had there been no light on which to fix their course, they might have perished in the storm.

In 1883 John Henry Newman wrote a hymn, "Lead, kindly light, amid th'encircling gloom," which describes what it means to trust in the light.

Lead, kindly light, amid th'encircling gloom,
    lead thou me on;
the night is dark, and I am far from home;
    lead thou me on:
keep thou my feet; I do not ask to see
the distant scene, one step enough for me.

I was not ever thus, nor prayed that thou
    shouldst lead me on;
I loved to choose and see my path; but now
    lead thou me on:
I loved the garish day, and, spite of fears,
pride ruled my will; remember not past years.

So long thy power hath blest me, sure it still
    will lead me on,
o'er moor and fen, o'er crag and torrent, till
    the night is gone;
and with the morn those angel faces smile,
which I have loved long since, and lost awhile.[1]

When one truly trusts in God's Light, Jesus Christ, one does not ask to see the future, "the distant scene." One knows that in life's most tragic moments of despair, though one should stumble, God's Light leads on step by step. Newman understood that trusting in the Light in this manner was very different from the time in his life when he trusted himself to shed light on his own path. Then, he trusted his pride, for it ruled his will.

Everyone who trusts the Light, keeps the focus of all life on the Light, and like the seaman, who might be lost at sea were it not for the light, stays on course through rough waters to safety. There may be anguish, fear, anxiety, and pain, but with a keen focus on the Light, God sees you through. You can trust in the Light!

Another hymn which uses the light metaphor in this way is Philip P. Bliss's "Brightly beams our Father's mercy," but it turns our attention to those along the shore who have become keepers of the light to direct others through times of distress to safety.

Brightly beams our Father's mercy,
    from his lighthouse evermore;
but to us, he gives the keeping
    of the lights along the shore.

Refrain:
Let the lower lights be burning!
    Send a gleam across the wave!
Some poor fainting, struggling seaman
    You may rescue, you may save.[2]

When singing this hymn, one tends to focus on the saving quality of
the light to rescue the lost, but the third line of the first stanza is powerful for the idea of witnessing with one's life through resistless love.
Bliss reminds us that we are the lighthouse keepers. It is through our
stewardship of the light that others are given guidance, be it in time
of rough or calm seas.

When the psalmist prays to God in time of trouble, one petition
resounds:
    O send out your light and your truth;
        let them lead me;
    let them bring me to your holy hill
        and to your dwelling. (Psalm 43:3)

God has sent out the light across the ages and has made us keepers
of the light that through our lives we might continue to beam forth
God's light, the light of redemptive, resistless love, to everyone in the
world. We are to let this light shine.

How Do We Let Our Lights Shine?

(1) *First of all, we open our hearts and lives to God's Light, Jesus
Christ.* We pray for God's Light in our lives. We pray this prayer:

> Ah, give me other eyes
>   than flesh and blood supplies,
> spiritual discernment give;
>   then command the light to shine,
> then I shall the truth receive,
>   know by faith the things Divine.

> For this I ever pray,
>   the darkness chase away
> from a foolish, feeble mind,
>   humbly offered up to thee;
> help me, Lord; my soul is blind,
>   give me light, and eyes to see.[3]

We must have light in our lives that makes our own pathway clear. God has not created human beings to live in darkness, but to live in the joy of the divine light which is love. Indeed, this is God's desire for all creation. Love is the sustaining light of the human spirit and of the whole creation. God is love and God is light. God has shed love light abroad through the gift of Jesus Christ, who comes and says with his life, ministry, death, and resurrection that God's sustaining, caring, empowering love is what gives life its meaning. Without such love there is no light for our way. We must decide to walk in the light of Christ's love and to be a servant of love. We must decide to follow Christ. The children's chorus "Give me oil in my lamp, keep me burning; keep me burning till the break of day" is a constant invitation to decide to follow the Light of all lights, Jesus Christ.

We must decide that we want to be filled with Christ's love, to personify self-giving, resistless love all our days. God has already claimed us with this love light before we could ever claim it ourselves. It is like a city set on a hill. It cannot be hidden. So it must be in our lives. God's love must be as permanently positioned in our hearts and souls, in our entire being, as a city built on a hill. When it is there, no one can overlook it, unless we try to keep the love light for ourselves alone.

Why did Jesus suggest that you cannot hide the city on the hill and that you do not light a lamp and put it under a bushel? Because there are those who wish to keep the love light to themselves. But the light under the bushel goes out.

After his conversion experience, when Charles Wesley knew that he finally stood by faith alone, he asked himself what every follower of Jesus should always be asking:

> And shall I slight my Father's love
>> or basely fear his gifts to own,
> unmindful of his favors prove,
>> shall I the hallowed cross to shun,
> refuse his righteousness to impart
>> by hiding it within my heart?[4]

Shall one refuse to share God's love with others by hiding it within one's own heart? Love not shared can never be resistless.

(2) *Secondly, we let our lights shine by walking in God's light, the light of divine love.* If we want to emanate God's love, we must commit ourselves to the discipline of human experience through which love is understood, interpreted, and integrated into our being. This means four things in particular that enhance the resistlessness of God's love in us.

(a) Make a commitment to serious study of the Holy Scriptures and other literature that enhances the knowledge and understanding of God's creation and redemption.

(b) Seek fellowship with other Christians in word, deed, and sacrament.

(c) Do what love does—always act out of love.

(d) Pray daily to be a personification of Christ's love.

If we want to let our lights shine with resistless love, do what St. Paul says love does: be patient and kind, do not be envious, boastful, arrogant, or rude. Do not insist on your own way. Do not be irritable or resentful and do not rejoice in wrongdoing, but rather rejoice in the truth. Believe, hope, and endure all. This is how others should describe our demeanor. If we do not do these things, the full image of Christ's love has not been formed in our hearts. If we do not respond in these ways, it does not matter how much we know, or how strong we think our faith is—we are nothing, for love is everything!

This is the heart of witnessing with our lives through resistless love: *be and do what love does!* If the love vision does not become an integrated part of our whole human experience, it will make little difference what we proclaim with words. Albert Outler averred that "the difference between healthy and unhealthy evangelism has less to do with the fervor of [one's] faith or the pure truth of [one's] doctrines than with the quality of [one's] love for others."[5] Therein lies the power and sustenance of witness.

(3) *Thirdly, we light up the entire house.* If we would let God's love light shine through us, we must place the light on a lampstand so that it will give "light to all in the house." Here there must be clarity as to what this means in terms of personality, character, behavior, and relating to others. Jesus does not mean that we place our "love lights" on display. Rather, the love of God opens the human personality so that it may share with others in the depth of human experience. The light of love in our lives is to light the paths of others and our own way. It is to shed the warmth of the rays of God's love wherever we go. Such warmth can overcome the coldness of relationships with others and give light to others who are wandering in darkness. This may happen when we least expect it. Often we will not know whether others have been warmed by the love light of our lives or have found their way through and out of the darkness because of that light. But we can be assured in our own hearts that, if we are filled with the light of God's love and truly become personifications of God's love, others will not be able to overlook our loving actions and behavior. This is precisely what Charles Wesley meant when he spoke of Elizabeth Blackwell's resistless love.

During many years of living in central Europe, I was struck as I rode through cities and villages at night that some houses and apartments would have their shades pulled down tightly so that you could not see easily whether a light was burning inside. In other dwellings, lights would be burning brightly and shades raised and curtains opened wide. The closed windows are like those who put their lighted lamps under a bushel, as if to retain all the light only for those inside. The dwellings with widely opened curtains and blinds revealing their brightly burning lights seemed to say to all that passed by, "Welcome, our home is a place open to all and for all to see. Our light shines out into the world and to all who pass by." When we let our lights shine, we must be willing to "light up the entire house." Who makes up "the entire house"? Those in our family, those with whom we live, those with whom we have daily contact. John Wesley comments on the light in our lives this way:

> If ye are thus holy, you can no more be hid than the sun
> in the firmament; no more than *a city on a mountain*

[probably pointing to that on the brow of the opposite hill]. Nay, the very design of God in giving you this light was that it might shine.[6]

(4) *Fourthly, we let our lights shine by being cheerful.* Cheerfulness does not come easily to some people, who seem to see the negative side of everything first, and there may be deep psychological reasons for such negativism which require sound counsel by trained persons. One thing is certain, God's love should not produce dreary, negative personalities who have no interest in bringing joy into the lives of others. On the contrary, God's love anchors joy in the human soul. This is not to suggest that God's love exempts us from the often very heavy consequences of human experience. This God does not promise. We are given the assurance, however, that the faithful may sow in tears but they will reap in joy (Psalm 126:5). "Weeping may linger for the night, but joy comes with the morning" (Psalm 30:5).

You have no idea how many people you may evangelize with a cheerful demeanor and a smile. Here we do not mean glib superficiality and conversation which effervesces with pleasant nothingness but rather deeply rooted joy which helps us to celebrate our lives and those of others. Cheerfulness is a primary trait of those who walk in the light of God's love. Note the words in the following stanza of John Wesley's eloquent English translation of Gerhard Tersteegen's German hymn:

> O Love, how cheering is thy ray!
>> All pain before thy presence flies!
> Care, anguish, sorrow, melt away
>> where'er thy healing beams arise.
> O Jesu, nothing may I see,
>> nothing hear, feel, or think, but thee![7]

God's love cheers. Pain, care, anguish, sorrow cannot endure the healing beams of God's love. It melts them away, and this is why Wesley says that he wants everything in his being and experience to be permeated with such love. He wants to hear, feel, and think God's love. Can one help being cheerful when so filled with love?

Some of the other stanzas of this translation by John Wesley describing what it means to walk in the light of God's love are among the most eloquent in the English language. God's love is the constant flame which gives light to one's life. It gives light and warmth to all around.

> Jesu, thy boundless love to me
>   no thought can reach, no tongue declare;
> O knit my thankful heart to thee
>   and reign without a rival there.
> Thine, wholly thine alone, I am;
>   be thou alone my constant flame.
>
> O grant that nothing in my soul
>   may dwell, but thy pure love alone!
> O may thy love possess me whole,
>   my joy, my treasure, and my crown.
> Strange flames far from my soul remove,
>   my every act, word, thought, be love.
>
> In suffering be thy love my peace,
>   in weakness be thy love my power;
> and when the storms of life shall cease,
>   O Jesu, in that important hour,
> in death, as life, be thou my guide,
>   and save me, who for me hast died.[8]

What a description of resistless love! It means full commitment, says Wesley. "O may thy love possess me whole" and may "my every act, word, thought be love." When love possesses one wholly, one will evangelize at the most unexpected moments of life without a word, for one's purpose will be to "be love" in one's body language (facial expression, touch, embrace), demeanor, actions, investment of time and resources, and presence. One's language will be affected and how one speaks will be filled with love. One's witness will be powerfully extended, because at the times when one is not consciously verbalizing the witness, one will be sharing the gospel and often unaware that others are being drawn to the resistless love light of Christ through one's presence and behavior.

8. Salt
Personifying Love: Matthew 5:13

Salt is another metaphor used by Jesus for the quality of the Christian's life. It is a metaphor essential to our understanding of witnessing with one's life. The affirmation "You are the salt of the earth" (Matthew 5:13) is used by Jesus in reference to the nature of one's being—one seasons the lives of those with whom one comes in contact. One's life so enriches the lives of others that they experience the reality of the psalmist's words, "O taste and see that the Lord is good" (Psalm 34:8).

Some years ago I had the privilege of meeting two indigenous Protestant pastors from Tibet. Both had been ordained when they were over sixty years of age. They came from a village high in the mountains where there is a small Christian community. They explained that in their village there were Buddhists, Christians, Hindus, and Muslims living harmoniously side by side. I inquired of one of the pastors, "How do you witness to your faith in that context?" He explained that he found Jesus' affirmation, "You are the salt of the earth" to be the most helpful image for witnessing in his situation. "It is my desire that my Buddhist, Hindu, Muslim, and Christian friends have their lives enriched by my presence. So I celebrate my life in Christ among them as a friend and helper. That is my best witness—to be salt that has not lost its taste." I inquired further, "How does this work out in daily living?" "Quite simply," he said. "For example, when my friends of other faiths need help of any kind, I help them as a servant of Christ. When they have special holy day celebrations, they invite me to share in their festivities and I invite them to share in our Christian holy days." Finally, I asked, "How can you be faithful in your discipleship to Jesus with such a lifestyle?" The pastor replied, "Jesus did not qualify his statement by saying that you are the salt of the earth for only one group of people or one part of creation. He said, 'You are the salt of the earth.' He wants me to season the lives of all my friends with the spirit of his self-giving love. I became a Christian and a pastor late in life and most of my friends in the village I have known all of my life. You must live in such a context in order to understand it fully, but I can do more to witness to my faith in Jesus where I live by being the salt, seasoning others' lives with his loving Spirit, than I can ever do with words."

There is tremendous wisdom in the words of this pastor about what it means to be the "salt of the earth." This metaphor shaped his proclamation of the Good News of the gospel where he lived. It formed his Christian lifestyle and witness.

Being the Salt of the Earth

(1) To "be the salt of the earth" means that it matters who you are! It is much easier to understand more tangible statements about identity. You are flesh and bone. You are body and mind. You are male. You are female. You are Filipino, Chinese, American, Native American, Irish, etc. One can be very specific about cultural, ethnic, and national identities. If someone were to ask you who you are, and you answered by saying, "I am the salt of the earth," you would probably get a very strange look from that person.

"Being the salt" is not about ethnic, cultural, national, or gender identity. This is a quality of human nature which cuts across all other tangible and obvious aspects of identity. When you look at processed salt and sugar in like bowls on a table, you cannot tell which is salt and which is sugar merely by looking at them. You will have to taste them in order to know. So it is with your identity as "the salt of the earth." By simply looking at you one cannot determine the nature of your being, but when you give of yourself to season the lives of others, they taste your enriching qualities.

Indeed, it matters who you are. It is who you are, the nature of your being, that determines how you relate to God, others, and the world.

(2) To "be the salt of the earth" means that you are imbued with the qualities of love, compassion, kindness, tenderness, humility, forbearance—those qualities of human personality and character so powerfully expressed in the life and ministry of Jesus. These aspects of human nature are the barometer by which you may judge how well seasoned you are as "the salt of the earth." What is unequivocally

clear from the life of Jesus is that one's entire nature must be love.

The hidden qualities of life, which cannot always be overtly identified, are often the strongest proclamation of the gospel, especially when words are of little use. The Christians of China are exemplars of this reality. The missionary enterprise in China of the nineteenth and twentieth centuries, Roman Catholic and Protestant, is an amazing story of the efforts of William Morrison, Hudson Taylor, and many missionaries from mainline churches and other groups.

In 1949, with the communist takeover of China, all missionaries were expelled within two to three years. Soon not a single missionary was left in the country. With the advent of the Cultural Revolution from 1967 to 1976, persecutions of all religions were prevalent. Churches were closed and pastors were sent to the villages to till the soil and to factories as laborers.

In 1949, there were 700,000 Christians in China. After the Cultural Revolution, the churches gradually began to reopen and pastors began to return to their former assignments. In 1997, the leaders of the Christian church in China estimated that there were about 10,000,000 Christians in China. During the years of the Cultural Revolution, verbal proclamation of the gospel was forbidden and, hence, it had no avenue of public appeal. To what then may one attribute the phenomenal growth of Christianity in China during these years? Christians stood as one with their fellow citizens—shoulder to shoulder, side by side; they worked, suffered, and endured. They could not proclaim the gospel with their lips, but they could proclaim it with their lives. They had learned from Jesus that the way of the cross is redemptive, and as they lived this out, others saw in them signs of hope. There are endless stories of day-to-day heroism. Thousands of people saw in the lives of the followers of Christ a quiet, loving endurance that drew them closer and closer to Christ himself. Such love was resistless, and millions were drawn to Christ through it.

This is one of the greatest stories of witnessing without words in the twentieth century. When you go to China today and worship in the churches, they are overflowing with people.

(3) *To "be the salt of the earth" means that it matters how you season, how you affect, the lives of others.* Some people do all of their cooking by following the recipes in cookbooks. Others cook based

on experience and instinct. Regardless of the method, clearly "too much salt can spoil the soup." So it is with our lives as "the salt of the earth." Finding a balance in seasoning the lives of others is an important and challenging task for every follower of Jesus. John Wesley expressed it this way:

> Ye—not the apostles, not ministers only; but all ye who are thus holy, *are the salt of the earth*—are to season others.[1]

Imagine for a moment that our lives are like a salt shaker. The salt in the shaker has not lost its taste, but it is trapped therein. If the shaker is never opened or shaken to let the salt flow out to enrich the taste of the food, no one will ever know whether or not it is any good. Inside the shaker it can season nothing. As "the salt of the earth," we too have to break open our lives so that the redemptive love of Christ that savors our lives can enrich the taste of life for others. The salt must be put to use or it serves no purpose. If we live self-contained lives, immured within ourselves, we too serve no purpose.

Retaining the Savor of the Salt

If salt no longer tastes like salt, who is to say that it is salt? As the salt of the earth we must retain the savor of Christ's love in our lives. It is possible for salt to lose the property which identifies it, namely, its flavor. Jesus says that when this happens, "It is no longer good for anything, but is thrown out and trampled underfoot." Can he possibly mean that human beings can lose their taste for God's love? The Scriptures aver that human beings can be so corrupt that they do not wish to be seasoned by God's love and have no desire to "taste and see that the Lord is good." The prophet Jeremiah once declared, "The heart is deceitful above all things, and desperately wicked: who can know it?" (Jeremiah 17:9, KJV). History testifies to the veracity of the prophet's statement. The story of humankind is full of war, violence, greed, conspiracy, and intrigue.

As promising as is Jesus' affirmation, "You are the salt of the earth," it is also a warning to every generation: you can lose the very thing that is the property of your identity—namely, the taste with which God seasons your life, which is love. Jesus gave a new commandment about this very matter: "You shall love one another as I have loved you." If you are seasoned by self-giving love, you avoid being "good for nothing but to be thrown out and trampled underfoot."

The story of Goethe's *Faust* relates the perpetual temptation of human beings to sell their "souls" to the devil for something they treasure more than God's self-giving love. Among the twelve disciples of Jesus, there was one named Judas who was also tempted in this manner. On the mountainside near the Sea of Galilee, he had heard Jesus utter the words about being the salt of the earth. He even continued to follow him after that occasion. Yet when the choice came between his own desire, his own greed, and following the Messiah, he chose himself and greed, and the salt of his life lost its taste. Judas savored money more than the love of Jesus. When God's love became expendable to him, his own self-destruction deprived his life of meaning. In Judas, the tasteless salt of the earth being trampled underfoot became a reality.

How Can We Be "The Salt of the Earth"?

(1) *We must be seasoned with God's redemptive love in Jesus Christ, which is what gives the salt of our lives its flavor.* We make the commitment to be filled with self-giving love throughout our entire life and to be seasoned by a loving, Christlike spirit. We are willing to let all that we do be tempered with love.

(2) *We must open our lives to others that they may be seasoned by the taste of the love of God we have experienced* and season our thoughts, words, and deeds with this love.

(3) *We must be discriminating in emptying ourselves for others.* St. Paul admonished the church at Colossae that we cannot season the lives of everyone. Be the salt of the earth where you are. Do not spread yourself too thinly, for salt spread too sparsely is almost tasteless. Also, exercise discretion. Just because your salt has not lost its flavor does not mean that everyone needs large doses of it at every moment. Remember, too much salt spoils the soup. Love, which gives the salt its flavor, does not insist on its own way. It is considerate and kind. Whatever you do or say, let it be out of love. Make this

the measure of how you season the lives of others and you will find the right balance. This is a vital dimension of the discipline of resistless love.

Fortunately, history is not only a story of war, violence, greed, conspiracy, and intrigue. It is also the story of hope, compassion, healing, and caring, for there are those in every age who season the world and those about them with love. They catch a glimpse of the enduring quality of self-giving, resistless love and they choose not to be self-destructive but rather to build up. They witness daily with their lives to the reality that "the salt has not lost its taste." They raise anew the question: How can we in our own time "be the salt of the earth"?

9. Stones
The Firm Foundation: Habakkuk 2:11

How is it possible for an inanimate object to be a witness to the gospel of Jesus Christ and to summon others to be servants of God's love? That does not fit into our scheme of logic in a world "run by human beings," in a world where they are the "superior intelligence." Yet, when the prophet Habakkuk wrote the words "These stones will shout!" (Habakkuk 2:11; see also 1 Peter 2:1–10 and Luke 19:28–40), he was reminding people in all ages that even stones can proclaim the gospel and witness to the enduring love of Jesus Christ in ways we may not expect. I was reminded of this as never before, when I made a trip to Russia a few years ago. I traveled to Sovietsk in the Kaliningrad-Oblast area of Russia, which was once the city of Tilsit in East Prussia and adjacent to the border with Lithuania, the northeasternmost part of Germany before World War II. For over fifty years, the area has been occupied by Russians, and only rarely does one find a native East Prussian.

I was searching for the Immanuel Church of the *Evangelische Gemeinschaft,* a European counterpart of one of the churches, the Evangelical Church, which united with the Church of the Brethren in the USA to form the Evangelical United Brethren Church, which subsequently united with The Methodist Church in 1968. The Immanuel Church was once an imposing structure that was built on property located at the address Querstrasse 5 & 6 (the old German name, but now called *Kossina ulitsa* in Russian), directly across the street from a large gymnasium, or college preparatory high school. When I arrived at the address, I found an empty lot. Hoping to acquire some information about the church, I went to the office of the school to inquire. One of the women told me that she had a colleague on the staff who could tell me something about the church. She telephoned her, and within a few minutes the colleague appeared.

The moment I asked about the church, she energetically began her story. "In June of 1958, I and some of my classmates were instructed by the school officials to tear down the rest of the church building (only the ground floor and tower were still standing at the time), in order to use the stones to build a workshop for the school. I will never forget that day," she said, as she held up her left hand and pointed to a scar on it. "I received a terrible cut, right here on my hand, as I picked up one of the stones, and it bled and bled. I bear the mark of that church on my hand."

I immediately thought of Habakkuk's words in the Hebrew Scriptures referring to the testimony of the ages to God's presence: "These stones will shout" (2:11). I remembered also Jesus' words to those who wanted him to silence those who were praising God so loudly on the day of his triumphal entry into Jerusalem: "If they are silent, the stones will cry out" (Luke 19:40).

As this woman used her scarred hand to point out the window toward the workshop that had been built with the stones from the Immanuel Church, these words of scripture had never been so alive for me. The stones that had surrounded the joys and sorrows of generations before, that made up the chambers of resonance for the proclamation of the word and joyous praise in song, whose surfaces had been trodden by the feet of children and the elderly and had embraced the worship and communal life of many people in this city formerly known as Tilsit—those stones were crying out through a scar-marked hand, through a workshop ringing with the laughter of youth and the clang of the tools of maintenance workers. Those stones were shouting: "We are still here! We still hear the pain and sorrow of the people. We still hear their laughter and joy. We are still here. We have not forsaken you!" And I thought I heard them say, "Do not forsake us!"

All the years that the lot stood empty it must have seemed as though the Immanuel Church had vanished from the city map of Sovietsk. But the stones once rejected became the foundation stones of a school workshop. They were still there and they were shouting.

Stones Tell a Story

Early in my professional career I studied archeology and worked on excavations in Greece, Jordan, and Israel. One thing I learned very quickly is that the stones you excavate or dig up have a story. In archeology this is literally true, for stones were used by ancient peoples to record their battles, victories, laws, and business transactions. They were shaped into tools and made into wheels. Sometimes they were inscribed with an artistic portrayal of a story from the life of the people.

On one occasion, the excavators at the ancient city of Geza were doing their work in a rather unusual way, namely, with a bulldozer, because they did not have enough money to continue excavating for many seasons. In this process, a large trash heap was created from the dumped dirt of the bulldozer. Sifting through the rubble, one of the persons working at the "dig" came upon one of the most important finds of the entire excavation. It is now known as the Geza Stone and tells the story of the ancient Assyrian Monarch Sargon I and his movement into that part of Palestine. The Geza Stone was the first evidence ever discovered that he had come that far into Palestine in his conquests.

Stones tell a story. The Geza Stone tells an important story of the Assyrian King Sargon I. But there are stones with stories other than those which are inscribed. They seem to be silent stones upon which no one has written, drawn, or hewn an image.

There are stones which know your story and mine. They know our inmost thoughts, our secrets. They have heard our crying and sighing in the night. They have heard our bursts of anger and laughter. They know us as well as, if not better than, anyone else. What if the stones in our houses or apartments should cry out? What stories would they tell?

There is an old Methodist Episcopal church building in Kaunas, Lithuania, which was built in 1910, dedicated in January of 1911, and confiscated by the Soviets after the Russian takeover of Lithuania in 1944. It became a Roman Catholic Church, a warehouse, a club, a movie theater, and finally a sports club. Now Christians (United Methodists) are worshiping there once more. Think of the stories the stones in that church building could tell—of some who still live in Kaunas and others who have gone on to their Maker. These are not only stories of Christians called Methodists and their rich heritage in that place. These are the stories of many who had no connection with the church.

What stories will they tell in the future? They will tell stories about a faithful band of Christians called Methodists who never gave up hope that God would one day let them return to worship in their church. They will tell stories about people who had no connection with the Christian faith, but who heard about the faithful band and came to worship with them and discovered new meaning in a daily walk with Christ. They will tell the stories shaped by everyone within their walls.

It is extremely important how we shape the story the stones will tell. What will our children and their grandchildren know about our stories here and in the next century? Will they tell the story of those who care so much for people and community that they give of themselves completely in service to one another, as Christ did among those with whom he came in contact from Samaria and Galilee to Jerusalem and beyond? If the stones should call us by name and reveal the desires of our hearts and lives, what would they relate? What would their witness be?

Present and future generations shall know of our witness to Christ and to love that reclaims lives at all costs, because the stones of our homes and our houses of worship were laid and resound with the shout: "God cares, God loves! We care, we love! Christ shows us how to care and how to love with resistless love!"

Stones are not eternal—God is

Yet, they seem so permanent. We know that if foundation stones are poorly laid, the structure built upon them will eventually develop imperfections which could lead to severe damage and possible destruction. So building codes are established and people trained in architecture and construction are authorized to inspect the way foundations are laid.

Nevertheless, earthly stones are not eternal. If you go the great pyramids of Egypt, built to house the bodies of Pharaohs and their families for eternity, you will see the windswept, worn faces of the stones and statues, some of which are no longer recognizable. If you go to the Grand Canyon and take a boat ride down the river at the bottom of the canyon, you will look up at the stone walls that have progressively been worn away by the rushing waters. If you go to Athens, Greece, you will see that the breathtaking Parthenon atop the magnificent Acropolis has been slowly worn away by wind and weather, and the female figures supporting the porch of the Erechtheum are slowly disappearing.

Stones are not eternal—God is. The psalmist refers to God as the rock of our salvation. "The rock" is also one of the names for God in the Book of Deuteronomy:

> The work of the Rock is perfect,
>   and all the ways of the Rock are just.
> God is faithful, without deceit,
>   just and upright. (Deuteronomy 32:4)

Hannah exclaims in her prayer found in 1 Samuel 2:2:

> There is no Holy One like the Lord,
>   no one besides you;
>   there is no Rock like our God.

David's Song of Thanksgiving in 2 Samuel 22:2–3 declares:

> The Lord is my rock, my fortress, and my deliverer,
>   my God, my rock, in whom I take refuge.

God is the eternal rock who forms the sure foundation for our lives. God the rock gives us constancy, security, stability, and endurance. Hence, we pray with the psalmist:

> Hear my prayer, O God;
>   listen to my prayer.
> From the end of the earth I call to you,
>   when my heart is faint.
> Lead me to the rock
>   that is higher than I;
> for you are my refuge,
>   a strong tower against the enemy.
>   (Psalm 61:1–2)

We remember St. Paul's words to the church at Corinth:

> I do not want you to be unaware, brothers and sisters, that
> our ancestors were all under the cloud, and all passed
> through the sea, and all were baptized into Moses in the
> cloud and in the sea, and all ate the same spiritual food,
> and all drank from the same spiritual drink. For they
> drank from the spiritual rock that followed them, and the
> rock was Christ. Nevertheless, God was not pleased with
> most of them, and they were struck down in the wilder-
> ness (1 Corinthians 10:1–5).

Let us drink from the spiritual rock, Christ, and be faithful. Let us pray to be marked with the qualities of God our rock—faithfulness, constancy, endurance, steadfastness, unwearied perseverance.

Let us drink the water of life which springs from the eternal rock, God our Creator—Redeemer—Spirit, and become one with the rock eternal.

There is one stone in particular whose shout I should like to hear: the stone that was rolled away from the tomb in the early hours of the day of Christ's resurrection. I wonder what it would say to us? "Christ is risen, he is risen indeed! I was rolled away to let Christ out of the tomb. I was rolled away to let you into the tomb to experience the power of Christ's resurrected presence. I was rolled away so that you could come into the tomb and see that he is not here, and so that you would discover from now on and in all ages that Christ is alive in us. I was rolled away so that people would know that God's love, the rock of all ages, is alive in you from now into eternity."

The First Letter of Peter 2:1–5 adjures the church:

> Rid yourselves, therefore, of all malice, and all guile,
> insincerity, envy, and all slander. Like newborn infants,
> long for the pure, spiritual milk, so that by it you may
> grow into salvation—if indeed you have tasted that the
> Lord is good. Come to him, a *living stone*, though reject-
> ed by mortals yet chosen and precious in God's sight, and
> like *living stones*, let yourselves be built into a spiritual
> house, to be a holy priesthood, to offer spiritual sacrifices
> acceptable to God through Jesus Christ.

Become like Jesus Christ a living stone and shout eternally his story and praise.

The Stones You Leave Behind Witness to Your Own Story

When I was a boy, we used to receive pamphlets in Sunday school, each one with a picture on the front and a Bible story inside. One in particular stands out in my memory, for I was very puzzled by the picture. It was the picture of a beautiful lake with many people standing, sitting, and lying on the banks in what seemed to be a peaceful setting. There was one man, who clearly was lame and seemed somehow at the back of the crowd. This picture portrayed the story of the man at the pool of Bethesda who was lame and could not get into the waters, when they were troubled so that he might be healed. I remember thinking as a little boy, "This picture doesn't make sense. Why can't the man just lie down on his side and roll into the water?" That seemed like a very practical solution to a six or seven year old. It was not until I was a grown man and studying archeology in Israel that I realized what was wrong with the picture. I stood one day at the excavation of the Pool of Bethesda and suddenly the stones told me the story. The pool was at the bottom of a long series of stone steps, which would have been impossible for a person who did not walk to descend. Suddenly I understood why the man could not get into the water under any circumstances, unless someone carried him down those many stone steps. The stones that were left behind told me the story.

There is a tremendous lesson in stones for witnessing with one's life. They speak by form, shape, position, symbol. They speak when no one is any longer there. The stones with which you lay the foundation of your life and with which you build the dwelling of your life will tell others a story for generations to come—your story. They will reveal what you hold dearest, most enduring, and of highest value. They will witness when you are no longer here. What story will they tell? Hopefully it will not be the Book of Deuteronomy's description of a senseless nation:

> [They] have dealt falsely with God,
>> a perverse and crooked generation.

> They are a nation void of sense;
>> there is no understanding in them.

If they were wise, they would understand this;
    they would discern what the end would be....
Indeed their rock is not like our Rock;
    our enemies are fools.

                    (Deuteronomy 32:5, 28–29, 31)

You are building the house now. You are determining the witness of the future in every aspect of your life. Build for the witness of ages to come. Build upon the rock of Jesus Christ and his resistless love which endures and the foundation of your life will proclaim the gospel, though you never speak a word!

10. Appearance
The Impact of Presence: 1 Thessalonians 5

Clothing makes an important statement about who we are. Our clothes reveal much about our ethnicity and the cultures from which we come. The dress of indigenous peoples often identifies their background or country immediately. The feathers and beads of Native American dress, an Arab *kafia,* a Bavarian *dirndl,* a cowboy's chaps, diverse African headdress—these all tell us immediately something about their wearers' origin or cultural identity.

The contemporary advertising industry relies on the fact that clothes make a statement. "Clothes make the person," says one slogan. While the garment industry is often less concerned with ethnic identity and more with establishing a set "fashion" (which may have a variety of cultural and ethnic adaptations), certain designers' names, such as Ralph Lauren, Bill Blass, Tommy Hilfiger, and Yves St. Laurent, have become synonymous with stylish clothes that identify the wearer as being "in" for the season.

How often is a decision about what to wear a major source of anguish or even a quarrel between a parent and child or spouses? Yet, while part of the world's population enjoys the luxury of making decisions about what to wear, millions of children, youth, and adults go to bed and wake up night and day with the same clothes, the only clothes they have, if any. The question "What shall I wear?" goes much deeper than a concern with what clothes to put on today. When we think of those who have little or nothing, we are reminded of the absurdity of decisions we make about clothing.

Clothes Make a Statement

What we wear makes a statement about what we think of ourselves and others. Many people cover their bodies for religious reasons with certain kinds of dress, for they genuinely believe this is the most respectful way to maintain their moral purity and that of others,

and to honor God the Creator. One should be sensitive to these perspectives and not disrespect or ridicule people for dressing different-
ly. Their willingness to look different for the sake of their ideals
deserves our utmost respect.

St. Paul encouraged the people of the church in Colossae, and
people of all ages, to consider what they wear. He spoke in a figura-
tive manner, because he knew that we impact one another's lives.
Therefore, our appearance makes a difference.

*In speaking of how we project our presence to and among oth-
ers, Paul* asked with what posture and appearance will we clothe our
personalities and characters? Here are the kinds of clothes he sug-
gested: "Clothe yourselves with compassion, kindness, humility,
meekness, and patience." How we appear to others and how we act
in their presence are of utmost importance. Then St. Paul admonished
everyone to "abstain from all appearance of evil" (1 Thessalonians
5:22, KJV). How? Be compassionate, humble, kind, meek, and
patient. If we act with these qualities of behavior and they determine
our attitudes, our appearance will reflect that.

Clothes Can Be Deceptive

A person can be dressed in one fashion and act in another. Jesus
warned on one occasion: "Beware of false prophets, who come to
you in sheep's clothing but inwardly are ravenous wolves" (Matthew
7:15). In contrast with the fashion industry, he is saying: "The clothes
do not make the person!" Even those who wear the most elegant of
fashions from Christian Dior to Gianni Versace, the most colorful
and finely made garments of ethnic and cultural backgrounds, or the
dress of a religious group or order can betray the elegance, tradition,
and sincerity they wish to project by their attire. Project or portray
what people will with external garments, Jesus says, "You will know
them by their fruits" (Matthew 7:16). The clothes with which you
adorn your inner being, your spirit—your soul, will be seen by others. If you are clothed with hatred, greed, deception, malice, anger, or
jealousy, others will see the wardrobe of your soul.

The Clothing That Never Goes out of Style

Fashions may come and go, but there is one way you can clothe yourself that will never go out of style—"Above all, clothe yourself with love," says St. Paul. How marvelous the world would be if its people would clothe their being, outward and inward, in this fashion. Then they would be known by the fruits of love. What greater testimony can there be to the redemptive, self-giving love of Christ than this!

It is interesting how certain styles of clothes lead to alienation. There are those who are offended by leather jackets and tight leather pants laced with metal studs of all sorts. Others find the neat gray suit with shirt and tie, the dress of the so-called "establishment," distasteful. What about wrinkled shirts/blouses and dirty blue jeans "made stylish" by rips in the knees and the seat of the pants? What about someone's native dress that is totally alien to your style of life and dress? No matter how strong the social, economic, ethnic, and cultural lines drawn by the clothes people wear, there is one style of dress that "binds everything together in perfect harmony." It is the style which surpasses all others, never is out of date, is eternal, and breaks the barriers created by all other human styles of dress. You will know you are always "in style," when you "clothe yourself with love." You will be able to overcome all of the inhibitions you have about the dress of others and truly love them as God's own creations.

Getting Dressed with Love

Though getting dressed with love would seem to be a very simple matter, it is not. When you rise in the morning, however, there is an exercise you may try in order to raise your own consciousness about being clothed with love. As you put on each one of your garments for the day, imagine that each piece of clothing represents one of the qualities St. Paul mentions. Write them down on a piece of paper with the heading: "My Clothes for Today." The list should include: compassion, kindness, humility, meekness, patience, and love. Put the list in an obvious place so that you will see it as you are getting dressed each morning. While this is merely a symbolic exercise, it may help you to exhibit the qualities of Christian living that the clothes you are wearing symbolize.

Wearing the clothes of love can be a powerful witness without words. Fashion designers set the mode of clothing for the season and hope that people will follow the new fashions and buy them. Jesus set the mode of fashion for the clothes of the human spirit and character which transcend and surpass the products of any fashion designer in any age. When we wear the clothes of love, we follow Jesus' fashion.

Think of yourself as a "fashion setter," one who sets the latest style for those around you by wearing the clothes of love so convincingly and well that others will become followers of the one who designed them for you, namely Jesus Christ.

11. Touch
The Importance of Relationships: Luke 8:43-48

One of the most vital ways in which we witness with our lives to the gospel of Jesus Christ is through the sense of touch. Without uttering a word, we can convey disapproval, violence, anger, hate, confidence, trust, love, etc., through touching others.

While standing in front of a bank of elevators in a New York department store waiting for my turn to go to another floor, I noticed more than once a typical reaction from many people. An elevator door would open revealing a tableau of shoppers packed in like sardines. Perhaps there would be room for one or two people with some squeezing. A person would step into the elevator and, because it was so uncomfortably tight, would step out immediately and say, "I'll just wait for the next one." Some people can develop an obsession with space. They do not want to be crowded and touch others, which for them feels offensive. There is an American song entitled "Don't Fence Me In" which is an insightful commentary on American culture. It begins:

Oh, give me land, lotsa' land
Under starry skies above;
Don't fence me in.
Let me ride through the wide open country
That I love,
Don't fence me in.

The broad, open plains of the Midwest and West filled the early settlers with a deep appreciation for space and the expanse of nature. For centuries before them, this was a life perspective of Native Americans.

Colonialism was in part a way of solving the problem of overcrowding in Europe. A history of African tribalism also reveals that endemic to the African experience is a longing for external freedom

in nature, which is plagued by feuds over boundaries and the protecting of one's own locality.

Return for a moment to the opening illustration and compare the
picture of the elevators in a New York department store with that of
a Japanese railway station where people are hired to push passengers
into the cars of the trains. In same parts of Asia, the attitude toward
crowding and touching is somewhat different. Can you imagine the
reaction of New Yorkers or Londoners to someone pushing them into
a train or subway car?

Our inhibitions about touching and our obsession with protecting
private space indicate the need for examining witness through touch,
for it can hurt or heal in the name of the Christ to whom we witness
and whom we serve. There is a New Testament story (Luke 8:43–48)
of a woman with the problem of an endless flow of blood who
pushed her way through a crowd in order to touch the hem of Jesus'
garment, and in so doing she was healed. The picture of one with an
outstretched hand seeking healing is a picture of humankind in every
age. Such an outstretched hand wants to touch, feel, make contact,
and receive new strength for living.

Luke records that after the woman touched Jesus' garment, he
asked his disciples, "Who touched me?" Jesus' question has become
our question as well. It is a vital one for witnessing to the gospel with
our lives.

We may not realize it, but for as long as we stay in a certain
place, we will have been proclaiming the gospel in the way we touch
the lives of others. And we need to ask the same question Jesus
asked, "Who touched me?" Whose life was made whole, renewed,
reclaimed, given new strength because it came in contact with mine?

How can we become sensitive evangels of the gospel of Christ
in the way we touch the lives of those around us?

Be Available to be Touched

Jesus' question reminds us that we must be available to be
touched. It is through contact with others that new life flows from
one to another. Jesus did not isolate himself from the pressing crowd,
from society, nor may we.

Some years ago I was working on an archeological expedition at

Tel Nagila, Israel, in the Negev, the southern plain section of Palestine. We were located between Jerusalem and Beersheba. As we left our quarters at an agricultural school each morning, we drove north about eight kilometers partially on pavement and then along a winding, dusty road to the *tel,* a mound of ruins. Soon after leaving the school we could look out across the vast wilderness and see very little vegetation and no trees. As we reached the dirt road, however, and the *tel* came into view on the morning horizon, the only tree for miles around, which was on the top of the *tel* where we were excavating, could be seen standing like a mighty ruler above the flat plain in regal solitude. Numerous times, as I gazed at it in the early light of dawn, I thought of how it was like so many people who seek to stand alone in life. I thought, "What a pity, it serves no purpose. It just stands there." Then two hours or so later, after I had worked in the blazing Palestinian sun and could take a break under the shade of the tree, my attitude changed. The tree took on a new meaning from the first moment I touched its shadows. It was the contact with the tree's shadows that gave us both meaning. Apart, we meant little or nothing to one another.

We cannot be touched by others if we isolate ourselves from them. Yet people in every society hang out their signs of protection: No trespassing! Keep out! Private! Even our adherence to a British tradition that people's homes are their castles is indicative of a feeling that at home we are strictly cut off from the rest of the world.

Every day we live, some people are pushing through our crowded lives to touch us and receive strength from us like the woman who touched the hem of Jesus' garment. We are the mediators of Jesus' healing love in this world. If we are not there in the crowd, no one can touch us and be made whole by that love.

Be Aware of Being Touched

Jesus' question, "Who touched me?" shows us that even amid the throng surrounding him, he was not too preoccupied to be conscious of someone who touched him.

In the so-called "free world" of the West, we have the freedom not to be touched. We can shut others out if we wish, and when we do, our sensitivity to the outstretched hand in need slowly but surely vanishes.

During the Communist era in Eastern Europe, I made a number of trips to the former East Germany (DDR). One of those trips underscored the contrast between my own way of life and one where the freedom *not* to be touched, as precious and perilous as it may be, had been all but lost. An East German church official related to me the story of his recently procured visa to visit his dying brother in West Germany. Even though he had met all of the requirements for the granting of the visa, he was kept waiting and guessing until the final two days prior to his scheduled departure before he received an affirmative decision and the visa itself. He had to make innumerable trips and telephone calls to the respective offices over a period of two or three months. He said, "They tried to intimidate me until the very last moment before giving me an answer." That was a society where people were constantly aware of being touched to the extent that a variety of emotional responses such as apathy, resignation, withdrawal, fear, anger, and antagonism became hallmarks of their behavior.

How aware are we of those who reach out to touch us, or that when we have been touched, power has gone out from us? That power goes out from us assumes that we have a power to share, that we draw strength from a source of power beyond ourselves, namely God, who has promised that the God-Child, Jesus Christ, will live within us and give us strength for the needs of each moment. When we have opened our lives to this indwelling Christ, the power of resistless love can flow out to others who touch us without a word. Christ within us makes us ever aware of the needs of others.

The Surprise of Being Touched

Jesus' question "Who touched me?" reminds us of the surprise of being touched. There is nothing in the story to tell us of Jesus' anticipation of being touched. He asks inquisitively, if not with surprise, "Who touched me?"

We too may be touched when we least expect it. We may not have the faintest notion of someone's desire to extend a hand to touch us. That realization makes us sensitive to a frightening responsibility in living. Our influence is constantly being felt by others. Like the lone tree atop the excavation, our lives cast shadows in which others may take refuge from the heat and perspiration of living. Whether we know it or not, we are influencing others each day. We have the opportunity to be a positive, loving, and redemptive influence in the name of Christ, who brings wholeness when people touch, or we may be a negative influence creating barriers between people. We may be individuals others want to touch or those whom they loathe to be near. Worst of all, we may never know it, because we do not stop to take a look at ourselves and examine who we are, how we act, what we think, and where we are going—things which, according to the accounts of the four Gospels, were very clear to Jesus.

Being a steward of one's touch, one's influence, is an awesome task. Recently I had an experience which stressed this for me in a new way. I was standing at a pedestrian crossing waiting for the traffic light to change to green. I looked both ways, as I was taught as a child, and saw no cars. My first impulse was to cross the street, even thought the light was still red! As my impulse almost got the best of me, I saw a mother holding her child's hand directly across the street, patiently waiting for the same light to change. I mastered my impulse and stood still until the light became green. On that occasion I saw someone who was about to be touched by my influence, and I conquered the temptation to follow the impulse to disobey the law.

Often, even when we do not know it, we are being observed by others who are reaching out to touch us, looking for an example to follow. Perhaps someone else will buy the books we buy, spend their money the way we spend ours, go to the movies we attend, drink and eat as we do, because they followed our example, because they touched our lives, and we did not even know it happened. Will they be touched by resistless love in us, even when we are unaware?

A four-line poem attributed to a distinguished American football coach is poignantly relevant to all who may be surprised by how one touches the lives of others, especially children.

A noble man I want to be
A little fellow follows me.
I do not dare to go astray,
For fear he'll go the selfsame way.

While I was traveling in Kenya a few years ago, someone

touched me in a way I shall never forget. It was indeed a surprise. As can happen anywhere when one travels, I was robbed of all my valuables–passport, money, airline ticket, credit card—and I spent a number of frustrating hours with the Nairobi police trying to determine whether I had any recourse. Thereafter I went to the American Consulate to procure a passport. Through it all, I was inwardly devastated and berated myself with the thought: "How could you, the seasoned traveler, be so unintelligent as to have all of these valuables with you at the same time? You know they should have been in the safe at your hotel." I was at a low point mentally and deeply depressed.

After procuring my passport, I headed for the American Express Company to apply for a credit card replacement. When I crossed the street at one corner and proceeded toward the address I had been given, I felt something brush against my leg. I thought it must have been an animal, perhaps a dog, that had darted across the road between the parked cars. As I turned to see what it was, I looked down and saw a little man with a shriveled body, who had dragged himself across the street with a block of wood in each hand. His legs were withered, obviously paralyzed, and he moved about by dragging them along under him. I prayed, "Yes, God, you are right. I am a fool. I have anxiety about my possessions, 'things,' which were stolen and which I shall ultimately replace, but this man has been marked by a destiny that I shall probably never know." Suddenly the burden of my inner concern vanished and I was completely freed of all stress and anxiety.

I was surprised by another's touch that day, but I was also redeemed by it. I was touched by the resistless love of Jesus. Be prepared to be redeemed, reclaimed, freed by another's touch—yes, even the Savior's touch.

Respond to Being Touched

Jesus' question "Who touched me?" reminds us that we must respond to being touched. Jesus spoke a kind and healing word to the woman who reached out to touch him. "Your faith has made you whole. Go in peace."

Responses to touching are varied indeed. Films flooded with violence often display violent human touch. Pain is inflicted on another by physical contact, and commands like "Keep your hands off me!" and "Don't you touch me!" are woven into scenes of love and hate, hope and despair. Everyone can utter them: men and women, boys and girls, cowboys, gangsters, politicians, intellectuals, poor, rich, police, criminals.

Have you ever paid attention to the responses of people on streetcars, subways, trains, and buses who are accidentally bumped by another person as the vehicle sways, catching the riders off balance? Even when the person who has inadvertently stepped on someone's toes, landed in a stranger's lap, or bumped an unknown shoulder says, "Please excuse me!" the response from the victim is often hostile. It may be a stone face and a stare followed by a sneering grimace and the shaking of the head as if to say, "You idiot! Why don't you watch what you're doing!" It may be total apathy with no acknowledgment that the other person even exists. Sometimes is it a smile and a kind voice that says, "It's alright," or "Don't worry, I'm okay." "A word in season, how good it is" (Proverbs 15:23)!

Jesus' response to the woman who touched his garment was a reassuring word to send her on her way as she departed with a strength-renewed body. "Your faith has made you whole. Go in peace." The eighteenth-century English poet William Cowper eloquently described the scene and reminds us of our need to reach out and touch Jesus.

> She, too, who touched thee in the press
>   and healing virtue stole,
> was answered, "Daughter, go in peace:
>   thy faith hath made thee whole."
>
> Like her, with hopes and fears we come
>   to touch thee if we may;
> O send us not despairing home;
>   send none unhealed away.

We need to be healed by Jesus, but ours is also the heritage to respond as he did to those who touch our lives. By no means do we attempt to pose as Jesuses, but redeemed by him and filled with his spirit of resistless love and compassion we too can pour out ourselves in responses of kindness and healing to those who reach out to touch us.

Those who did not want to be touched by Jesus sent him to a criminal's death upon a cross. It is from that cross he reached out to touch our lives. Will we make ourselves available to be touched by him? Will we be aware of his cleansing touch and surprised by his unexpected, redeeming, outstretched, nail-scarred hands? Will we respond to his touch and depart in peace? Will our faith make us whole?

Some day we shall depart from this world. Before that departure it is imperative to ask, "Who touched me?" Who reached out to me for strength, to be made whole? What boy, girl, man, woman? What will the answer be? We cannot outguess destiny, but as the evangels of the Good News of resistless love who dare to touch the lives of others and dare to be touched, we can write history daily with our lives. When we have been touched by Christ, we can let ourselves be touched and touch others in a new way. With him as our healer, we too can mediate his healing, loving touch to others as a powerful witness.

12. Shadows
Stewardship of Influence: Psalm 91

There was an ancient Hebrew prophet, Jonah, who once sought refuge in the shade of a rubber tree plant, as he sat on a hillside in the blistering Near Eastern sun waiting for the fulfillment of the prophecy he had proclaimed to the people of Nineveh.

If you have ever sought refuge from the heat of the day, you know the sense of release found in the shadows cast by a tree, a plant, or a building. It is in this sense of refuge that Psalm 91 speaks of those who "abide under the shadow of the Almighty." In other words, God is a refuge and strength amid all the pressures of life.

One of the ways we witness is through the shadows we cast upon the lives of others. Perhaps what it means to abide in the shadow of the Almighty can best be understood by examining our own shadows. Like our Creator, we too cast shadows. We cannot stand in them ourselves but someone else can.

As a child, did you ever play with your own shadow in the moonlight or under a street light at dusk? You can move every conceivable way, but you cannot stand in your shadow or "catch" it. Everyone else can stand in your shadow but you.

We are all casting shadows of influence and others are standing in them, even when we do not know it. They hear our words, see our actions, observe our appearance. They experience the witness of our shadows on their lives.

Shadows of Gloom and Joy

We cast shadows of gloom and joy. We have the ability to make others feel miserable or uneasy by our grouchy dispositions and by character and personality traits which offend others. Maybe we don't have bad dispositions as such, but we can be nonresponsive to others, "pushy" and overbearing, inconsiderate and rude, or overly self-righteous and sanctimonious and cast shadows of gloom over the lives of those about us. Is this the kind of witness we want our shadows to be?

On the other hand, we can cast shadows of joy. On a dreary, rainy day, I once walked into a bank where I did business and went to the counter for currency exchange and one of the women, who often served me, greeted me cheerfully with a tremendous smile. I inquired, "How are you?" She replied, "Fantastic! I don't let the weather get me down like some people." Unknown to her I stood in the shadow of her smile for the rest of the day. Her shadow was a witness of joy, even though she may have been unaware of it.

I once had a friend who was bedridden with arthritis and who earned what little income she could by crocheting with fingers very badly disfigured by arthritis, a physical condition that would have made many people give up doing anything with their hands. As I entered her room on each visit, she greeted me with a broad grin and said, "Isn't it another grand day?" I always stood in the shadow of her joy long after departing.

The underlying truth and reality are that our shadows of influence are a powerful witness. What a responsibility we carry as followers of Jesus Christ, for we are to exhibit his demeanor of resistless love wherever we go. Think of it—we can make or ruin someone's day or someone's life on the basis of whether we cast shadows of gloom or joy. If we would witness to Jesus, we should cast shadows of joy on the lives of others.

Shadows of Indifference and Sameness

We can also cast shadows of indifference and sameness. Some of us never look back to see whether we are casting shadows. In our self-preoccupation, we are unaware that we are witnessing to that for which we stand, or to the One, Jesus Christ, for whom we stand. Such insular living makes us indifferent to others, their lives, and their needs.

There may be many in our communities and Christian churches who cast shadows of indifference upon one another by refusing to make the first move of friendship, to open the door. When we think of asking someone to take a walk with us, eat a meal together, or just talk, it is much easier not to do it, than to do it. When we do not take the step, we cast shadows of indifference and have not borne witness to a caring Savior who said, "Inasmuch as you did it unto one of the least of these, you did it to me."

Our shadows of sameness are similar to those of indifference. I was once talking with a friend in Germany who had recently moved there from North America. He said that living in another culture had made him suddenly aware of the shadows of sameness out of which he had come. He had lived in a lovely suburban community in a large city filled with business executives like himself—people who drove the same kinds of cars, had the same kinds of houses, dressed alike, had the same set of suburban values, and whose companies hired more and more of the same kind.

Shadows of sameness can be a deadly witness, for they can destroy God-given creativity and individuality. They pour us into a mold of conformity which has little or nothing to do with being god-like and a follower of Jesus.

We are all casting shadows and we are all standing in shadows. We cannot stand in our own shadows, but someone else can and will. We can cast shadows of good or evil, honesty or dishonesty, falsehood or truth, and so on. The shadows we cast shape lives and we are shaped by those in whose shadows of influence we stand.

What will those who stand in our shadows experience? Resistless love?

The Shadow of the Almighty

What impact does standing in "the shadow of the Almighty" have upon our lives? More than once we meet similar statements in the Psalms: "Keep me as the apple of the eye; hide me in the shadow of your wings" (Psalm 17:8). "How precious is thy steadfast love, O God! The children of earth take refuge in the shadow of your wings" (Psalm 36:7). The prophet Isaiah rejoiced that he was held in the shadow of God's hand (49:2).

According to Psalm 91, the impact of standing in God's shadow is that in God we have a refuge, protection, deliverance from fear and evil. "God has set [the divine] love upon me (Psalm 91:14, KJV)," says the psalmist. Dr. W. A. Shelton says in a comment on this verse, "Love begets love and responds to love."[1] That is why "we love, because God first loved us" (I John 4:19).

Beware, however! The psalmist is not speaking of a life insurance or accident policy. Standing in God's shadow, wherein we are covered by divine love, does not mean we are immune to temptation, difficulties, tragedy, failure, and death. Faith is not a guarantee against calamity!

The protection of which the psalmist speaks transcends the merely physical and external. Such protection comes through the reinforcing of our inner resources. It is knowing that the external cannot overpower the internal. It is here that we learn a very special lesson about witnessing without words. To have the inner assurance that our lives are indeed in God's care no matter what befalls us cannot be adequately put into words, but it can be lived. We can show the "tempers of the Lamb of God" in all aspects of our demeanor.

This is why the German theologian Dietrich Bonhöffer could walk calmly to his execution at the hands of the Nazis on April 9, 1945. Christ was his inner peace, a strength unwavering. This is the "truth unutterable" of which Charles Wesley often writes in his hymns and poems.

Many years ago my youngest son Mark and I went to a summer camp attended by Christians from about twenty-five different countries near Brno, Czechoslovakia (the country's name at the time) during the height of the Communist regime and the Cold War. In one of our first sessions together, we were divided into small groups to discuss three words: faith, hope, and freedom. One of the people in our group was a young Czechoslovakian soldier. I recall asking him what freedoms had been taken away from him as a result of the Russian invasion a few years before. His reply is implanted in my memory: "None. My freedom is internal. There is nothing they can take away from me. God reigns within me. That is the assurance and truth I know within me, but no words can express." He had discovered the meaning of standing in the shadow of the Almighty, which, in and of itself, is a tremendous witness to others.

God *is* our refuge, but we must be vigilant in prayer and fellowship one with another. There *is* a strength available for all from the God who is "the same yesterday, today, and for ever."

Alfred Lord Tennyson wrote in *Morte d'Arthur:*
More things are wrought by prayer
than this world dreams of.

But the dreams of the world are very different from those of the
psalmist, who hopes for a world whose security is sustained by standing in the shadow of the Almighty. What is the witness of world
economy and diplomacy across the ages? The pursuit of national and
international security reigns supreme in a world that measures the
worth of people according to what they can secure, protect, procure,
and consume.

If we stand in the shadow of the Almighty, we witness in all that
we do to our belief that there is a security greater than that of the
world. It is in God alone!

There is a witness we make by standing in God's shadow, which
infuses us with power. It makes the weakest of us strong enough to
face all obstacles. To those around us, our difficulties may seem more
than we can bear. Yet, when we stand in the shadow of the Almighty,
we know the inner peace of God's resistless love and draw strength
from St. Paul's words to the church at Rome, "If God is for us, who
can be against us" (Romans 8:31)!

In John Bunyan's *Pilgrim's Progress,* Timorous and Mistrust
encountered grave difficulties when they fled from the lions that
blocked their path. Christian, however, continued boldly confronting
whatever befell him and discovered that it was not as horrible as he
had imagined:

This hill, though high, I covet to ascend;
The difficulty will not me offend.
For I perceive the way of life lies here.
Come, pluck up, heart, let's neither faint nor fear:
Better, though difficult, the right way go
Than wrong, though easy, where the end is woe.
(I, chapter 3)

One of the early great country and western singers in the U.S.
was Jimmy Rogers, who had a very short-lived career (only five
years). When he died at age thirty-five, however, he had recorded

over 1,000 songs. His last album was recorded in a studio equipped with a bed, because he would become so exhausted after recording that he would have to lie down and rest. He knew death was impending from the crippling tuberculosis he suffered, but he did not resign himself to it. In his moments of agony he gave others joy for years to come. He cast a shadow of musical joy over generations of country and western music lovers yet to be born.

This is the kind of quiet, unverbalized strength God gives us that is indeed protection and refuge in calamity. Nothing can slay the inner life of faith and joy. It was this life and this joy that Jesus came to make clearer than had been done before him. He demonstrated with his life what the prophets and seers before him had said with words. He too was misunderstood in a world that wanted a different kind of security and protection than he personified. But he cast a shadow abroad throughout history—the shadow of the cross. When we stand within that shadow, we have a vantage point from which all of life's obstacles and petty cravings for security come into proper focus. We grasp that our own shadows should be an extension of the shadow of the cross (the symbol of resistless love), which witnesses to others, though we never say a word. We give ourselves for others as Jesus gave himself for us.

God's shadow is cast across the earth as a divine refuge for all humankind. Against the background of our own small world, we too cast shadows. We cannot stand in our own shadows, but someone else can. That someone will know, though we never speak a word, if we are standing in the shadow of the Almighty's resistless love.

Part 3

Personifying the Resistless Love of Jesus in the New Millennium

13. Justice and Piety
The Practice of Witness: Isaiah 58

In the 58th chapter of Isaiah, the prophet articulates some important qualities of life for the witness of resistless love. The true worship of God demands that one be true to oneself and God in faith and practice. It is not possible to practice righteousness for the wrong motives and be a faithful servant of God. "To be or not to be" the kind of person he describes—"that is the question!" While the prophet focuses pointedly upon many negative aspects of those who are evangels of falsehood in their religious practice, here is a paraphrase of the positive aspects of the prophet's plea that Israel be God's faithful witness through just living.

> A SONG OF JUSTICE[1]
> Isaiah 58
>
> Seek God, delight in God's way,
> keep God's law, be humble, and fast.
> Be righteous in all you do,
> yet, these things will never suffice.
> There is more to knowing God
> and knowing how to live
> than personal delight
> in righteous things you do.

DO JUSTICE, LOVE MERCY,
WALK HUMBLY WITH YOUR GOD.

God's fast is not mere fasting,
or doing without for your sake;
it is sharing yourself with others
and doing without for their sake.
It is loosing the bonds of the wicked,
setting oppressed workers free,
sharing your bread with the hungry
and giving the homeless a home.

DO JUSTICE, LOVE MERCY,
WALK HUMBLY WITH YOUR GOD.

God's fast means taking up
the yoke of all who have not,
whose lives are a constant fast
from the abundance of your own.
So be a light in the darkness;
do not hide from yourself:
Pour out yourself for others
and be a healing stream.

DO JUSTICE, LOVE MERCY,
WALK HUMBLY WITH YOUR GOD.

We have often heard the phrases "Say what you mean and mean what you say" but we have also heard that "actions speak louder than words"! The Holy Scriptures summon us to "being." Micah 6:8 pleads, "Do justice, love mercy, walk humbly with your God." This is a call to "being," to the personification of justice, mercy, and humility. While we may speak just, compassionate, and humble words, the prophet is bidding us to personify in the wholeness and fullness of our being God's justice in all we do.

It is often said somewhat glibly that "talk is cheap," but the decision to be a personification of God's loving justice on this earth is one to which the prophet Isaiah called the people of the earth centuries ago. The decision "to be or not to be" what God wants us to be is the most important one of our lives. The summons is not, however, to a mere perfunctory and mechanical observance of the prophet's admonitions.

Learn to Live in the Imperative

How can we "become" persons whose very essence is a daily witness to loving justice? *We must learn to live life in the imperative:* seek God, delight in God's way, keep God's law, be humble, fast, be righteous in all you do. Nevertheless, beware! Merely following the imperatives, though one must always live one's life in the imperative as a follower of Jesus Christ, is not enough. There is always the danger that one will take such pride in doing righteous things that they become a means of self-gratification. This is what it means "not to be" what God would have us "be."

How do you become a doer of justice, a lover of mercy, and one who walks humbly with your God? It requires conscious intent. For example, fasting can be personally cleansing, physically and spiritually. Self-denial can purge us of selfish desire. Nevertheless, if fasting is merely for personal discipline, it has not been taken to its greatest spiritual depths. To do without for your own sake is one thing. To do without for the sake of another is a fast which not only denies self but nurtures the lives of others. I recall how when I was a young boy, my father, a Methodist minister, encouraged days of fasting in the churches he served. Those fast days had a very specific purpose. I remember them well, for food is something youngsters often take for granted and something a growing boy can consume without a great deal of thought or effort. On fast days we were allowed to have a glass of tomato juice two or three times during the day, but that was all. But I have never forgotten that all were asked to give the money they would have spent for groceries on that day to missions. The idea that even I, a little boy, could give to someone who was hungry, provide a book for another child's education, or supply needed clothing through doing without food for that day is still powerfully embedded in my memory. I was learning to do justice, love mercy, and walk humbly with God.

In my hometown of Birmingham, Alabama, there is a statue of a kneeling man at the center of one of the busiest intersections of the city. This gentleman was a Presbyterian pastor, known affectionately by young and old as Brother Bryan. Though I never knew him, it was from him that I learned some of the first and most impressive lessons about what it means "to be" God's justice, love, and mercy where one is. I remember vividly a day I was riding with my father in our family car with the radio on. Suddenly, the broadcaster announced that it was now the appointed time, as decreed by the mayor of the city, for the wheels of all vehicles throughout this city of over 300,000 people to stop for fifteen minutes in memory of Brother Bryan, who had recently died. And so my father pulled to the curb, as all traffic came to a halt.

When I became a teenager, I began to work from time to time at the Brother Bryan Mission in the heart of the city. It was there I learned why the traffic in the city stopped to commemorate his life. This man so powerfully personified the loving justice of Jesus Christ everywhere he went in the city that he would give the coat from his back in the middle of the sidewalk to anyone in need, regardless of race or creed. No one's need was too great for him to attempt to meet it. He was a walking personification of witnessing with one's life. Whatever he did was a witness to the Good News of God's love for all humankind in Jesus Christ. Brother Bryan was resistless love personified.

Brother Bryan was pastor of the Twenty-Second Street Presbyterian Church. After he had served that parish many years and had had a powerful impact on the needy of the city, the Session of his congregation wanted to do something to honor him. They wanted to hang some sort of a sign outside the church that would let people who passed by know that this was Brother Bryan's church. Numerous suggestions were made by many members of the congregation. They were gathered and presented to Brother Bryan, who was asked to decide on one of the proposed texts for a sign. When he had been through all of them, he rejected every one. Then he informed the officials of the parish that there was only one sign that they could hang on the church to let people know that it was the place he served as pastor and the text of that sign must be only the verse of scripture: "God is love." And to this day, when you ride by that church, that is the sign you see.

Brother Bryan was the living evidence of God's love on earth. He said with his life—God is love! He became God's self-giving, self-emptying, resistless love to everyone who passed by.

We have said above that *we must learn to live life in the imperative*. As valuable as auxiliary or helping verbs are in our vocabulary, they can be devastating to our "becoming" nonverbal expressions of the Good News of God's love. Think of the difference between "should, could, would I" and "seek God, delight in God's way, keep God's law, fast, do righteous things, share yourself and your means with others, break bread with the hungry, give the homeless a home, loose the bonds of the oppressed." If I preface my inner thoughts with helping verbs, I will probably never "be" a personification of God's love. I will be tenuous, indecisive, and in so doing elect "*not to be*" rather than "*to be*" who and what God wants me to be. If I want to be God's resistless love, I must do what that love does. It does not act tenuously. It acts decisively. It acts justly.

Pour Out Your Life for the Needy

The prophet Isaiah also suggests a second and vital step toward "being" a personification of God's Good News of love. *Do not hide from yourself—pour out your life for the neediest of all.* The tendency of those "who have" is to live their lives raising a family, procuring a sufficient dwelling, educating the children, planning for "secure" retirement. While one may not wish to be a burden to one's family or society as a whole, the pitfall looms before societies of reasonably high standards of living that the population will live primarily for itself. One need only listen to and read leading politicians and economists as they discuss what is necessary for the health of a nation's economic future. The concern is usually more about what one can do for oneself than what one can do for someone else. According to the Holy Scriptures, this has absolutely nothing to do with "being" what God wants us to be. It is easy to breed fears and prejudice such as "Watch out for the strangers in our midst," "Don't let foreigners get our jobs," "We don't want *that* kind of people in our neighborhood," etc.

The prophet says, however, if you want to "be" a doer of justice, a lover of mercy, a humble walker with God, you must *pour out your life for the most unlikely.* In deciding "to be or not to be" what God wants you to be in your life, here is a primary step you must take.

Work to loose the bonds of the wicked by helping to set oppressed workers free. Those who *are* what God wants them to be are advocates of justice for workers who are enslaved to exploitive systems, economies, poor working conditions, low wages. They also share their bread with the hungry and they give the homeless a home. This is witnessing to resistless love with one's life. The word becomes flesh. Those who *have* take up the yoke of those who *have not.*

Some think that fasting is a tremendously difficult feat, because their bodies are conditioned to three meals a day. Giving up even one meal is almost unthinkable. Unquestionably one should not fast without thinking of proper nurture of the body with the daily required minerals and vitamins, or else one may damage one's health. But think of it for a moment. In one sense, to have the option to fast is itself a luxury. One denies oneself that which one has. Yet millions of children and adults do not have this option. They fast sometimes for days, if not weeks on end, because they have nothing to eat. Their bodies are denied the minerals and vitamins that prevent disease and death. Is it really so much to ask that we witness with our lives by fasting for the sake of others? Through denying ourselves, we take up the yoke of those who have nothing. We need utter no word whatsoever in order to feed a hungry child or adult.

We can do much to empower the nonverbal witness of our lives as followers of Jesus Christ by discovering the value of fasting. It is personally redemptive and cleansing. But it can be also an avenue toward social holiness, if it is practiced with a view toward service to others. Fast, yes, but fast with a purpose of self-giving service to others. Let your self-denial be a gift to others.

It is easy for some to fast for all of the wrong reasons, as the prophet delineates in Isaiah 58. It is pointless, as is most religious practice, if, as the prophet says, "you serve your own interest on your fast day" (58:3c). When, however, your fast is the offering of humble service yoking your life to those in need, you will meet your God face to face in strength. It is then that—

> The Lord will guide you continually,
>   and satisfy your needs in parched places,
>   and make your bones strong;
>   and you shall be like a watered garden,

like a spring of water,
whose waters never fail. (Isaiah 58:11)

Yes, in humble fasting we are yoked to others and to our Savior, though we never utter a word.

With fasting and prayer my Savior I seek,
and listen to hear the Comforter speak;
in searching and hearing thy life giving Word,
I wait thy appearing, I look for my Lord.[2]

Isaiah linked the spiritual act of fasting, the practice of piety, with becoming a just person in God's sight.

God's fast means taking up
the yoke of all who have not,
whose lives are a constant fast
from the abundance of your own.

It is in the practice of such justice that you encounter God. It is there you discover God's redeeming and saving presence.

One dare not forget Isaiah's declaration: "The Lord is exalted by justice" (5:16). In chapter 56, the prophet makes clear that justice and salvation are mutually indispensable: "Thus says the Lord: Maintain justice and do what is right, for soon my salvation will come, and my deliverance be revealed" (56:1). Doing justice, God says, heralds God's salvation and deliverance. What a powerful pattern for the church of Jesus Christ in its evangelization! Maintain justice and God's salvation will be revealed! Jesus reminds people of all ages that justice, mercy, and faith should be self-evident aspects of our spiritual formation and practice (Matthew 23:23).

The prophet Isaiah provides an important clue for understanding what it means to witness without words through deeds of justice! *Justice is indispensably bound to God's salvation.* Hence, those who follow God's incarnate way revealed in Jesus link their lives with justice and the announcement and reign of God's salvation. Therefore, Christians do not do merely "good" deeds or honorable humanitarian deeds; rather they do justice, which God expects (Isaiah 5:7), which declares: God saves! God delivers!—through the incarnate

Christ!

"'I love justice,' says the Lord, 'I hate robbery and wrongdoing'" (Isaiah 61:8). If you want to love what God loves, you will love justice! If you want to personify resistless love, you will *be* just!

When the prophet Micah announced what God requires of every human being, namely, "to do justice, and to love kindness, and to walk humbly with your God" (6:8), he did not place the priority on verbal articulation of justice but on *doing* it—on *being* just.

14. Beyond Ourselves
Inclusive Witness: Psalm 29, Numbers 22-24, John 4

Boundaries are a reality with which we live. When the ones prescribed by nature, the limits of the natural order, are overstepped, the consequences may be grave. In physics there are a variety of "laws" which seem to function as ultimate truths for all reality, such as Newton's law that for every action there is an equal and opposite reaction. There are laws or boundaries of gravity (at least on earth) and of weightlessness in space. If one attempts to drive around a curve faster than the limits of centrifugal force permit, one may wind up in a ditch, against a tree, or down a ravine. While some natural boundaries are ones over which we have little or no control, there are other boundaries which we create. Some of them are very personal; others are social, economic, political, racial, ethnic, cultural, and religious. The boundaries within creation are a constant, nonverbal witness to God's creative order. They are there and ongoing, whether we acknowledge them or not, and when we ignore them, we and all creation suffer.

The boundaries that human beings establish can also be a powerful nonverbal witness. For example, increasingly the boundaries drawn or set by people of religious persuasions are troublesome. There are the horrid realities of Belfast, Bosnia, Burundi, Kosovo, Rwanda. Yet, it is difficult to look beyond ourselves to a larger global, human, and religious reality, for we are the sum total of our experience.

For Jews, Christians, and Muslims, who are summoned to a common humanity under God as *people of a sacred book,* it is interesting that cultural and ethnic realities, boundaries if you will, determine in large measure the hermeneutic of faith and life, often with little regard for *the sacred book.* In the case of Christians, this has to do with what they receive and call the Bible or the Holy Scriptures, the Hebrew and Greek Scriptures.

Are there some clues within the Bible for the followers of Jesus that help them to see beyond themselves, who they are and where they are, to a different understanding of the world and others—help them to look beyond the boundaries which have such a powerful, nonverbal witness? Is it possible that this vision itself can evangelize those with whom we come in contact?

Biblical Vision

(1) *In the Bible, we discover that God's vision is always larger than any singular vision of humankind or community of faith.* Jews and Christians often espouse messianic views that conflict. Jews at various times have claimed that *Bar Kochba, Rabbi Akiba,* and the Jewish people as a whole are the Messiah. Christians, following the New Testament, have claimed that Jesus is the Messiah. It is interesting to note, however, that the only other person literally called a *mawshiah* (messiah) in the Holy Scriptures, apart from Jesus, is someone who stood outside of both the Jewish and Christian faith communities: *Cyrus the Medean King.* He it was who decreed that the Jewish people might return to their homeland from exile, and the prophet Isaiah called him a *mawshiah.* Isaiah saw God's redemptive action effected beyond the boundaries of the Jewish community of faith. The prophet calls one a messiah who is neither Jew, Greek, nor Jesus himself. Is this a parable for how we may look beyond ourselves to include in love those who are not like we are?

(2) *In the Bible, we discover a divine vision that extends beyond the bounds of Judaism and Christianity.* The poignant nature Psalm 29, though preceded by the heading "A Psalm of David," probably a rabbinical ascription from the middle ages, was discovered at Ras Shamra (in present-day Lebanon) in cuneiform script in a proto-Canaanite language form that predates King David. Is it strange that God's people would appropriate imagery, metaphors, and language that expressed their faith from the culture in which they lived? Is it strange that God revealed the nature of divine creation through the language and culture of the Israelites' immediate world? One can with integrity call this psalm "A Psalm of David," for it resonates the view of creation espoused in Davidic psalmody. Does it not strengthen the view of this sacred book to see it as a part of the life of the world in which it was born and received? The reality is that God's

word came to God's people from beyond the boundaries of the community of faith as it was known in the Hebrew Scriptures.

(3) *In God's vision within the Bible, the least likely diviner or sorcerer outside the community of faith may become a source of blessing for the faith community.* Chapters 22–24 of the book of Numbers tell the story of how Balaam, a diviner who worked for a fee and was engaged by Balak to place a curse upon Israel, became the source of Israel's blessing. There are those who would maintain that Gandhi of India lived out the "law of Christian love" more effectively in his native land than many Christians. The Bible teaches clearly that it is God's prerogative to reveal the fullest dimensions of divine love for creation in any way God chooses; hence, believers must be ever alert for the signs of God's realm in places they least expect to experience them.

(4) *In God's messianic vision of the Bible, it is interesting that the woman, a Samaritan, to whom Jesus actually revealed he was the Messiah was from outside the faith community.* In the Gospel of John, chapter 4, she expressed amazement that Jesus had asked her for a drink of water, since Jews had no dealings with Samaritans. It was not to the chief priests and scribes that he revealed he was the Messiah, but to someone with whom the Jews had nothing to do.

Are there clues here for an emerging Christology in the twenty-first century? In any century? The true identity of Jesus is not delineated by our cultural, ethnic, or religious reality. His identity is defined by who he was and by his life, ministry, death, and resurrection. He said almost nothing that had not been said before him by prophets, priests, and other rabbis. Perhaps his one innovative oration was the Sermon on the Mount (Matthew 5–7). But he is defined as messiah, for he personified messiah in thought, word, and deed.

Perhaps there are important clues for an emerging Christology here, for the authenticity and veracity of our Christology will be more effectively determined by how we personify who Jesus the messiah was and is than by who we say he was in theological and philosophical terms. But we must see with God's vision, which looks beyond self to others.

The Practice of Looking beyond Ourselves

Two aspects of worship life in the Wesleyan tradition may help us in this quest: *Holy Communion* and the *Love Feast*. The former celebrates that all are welcome at God's table, where all share in love and no one is a stranger. We are, as Daniel Migliore says, "a vulnerable guest awaiting the welcome of others."[1] At the heart of our Christology must be the motif *no one is a stranger*. Charles Wesley in his hymn entitled "The Great Supper" shapes this motif eloquently in reflecting on the parable told by Jesus in Luke 14.

1. Come, sinners, to the gospel feast:
    let every soul be Jesus' guest.
    Ye need not one be left behind,
    for God hath bid all humankind.

2. Sent by my Lord, on you I call;
    the invitation is to all.
    Come, all the world! Come, sinner, thou!
    All things in Christ are ready now.

3. Come, all ye souls by sin oppressed,
    ye restless wanderers after rest;
    ye poor, and maimed, and halt, and blind,
    in Christ a hearty welcome find.

4. My message as from God receive;
    ye all may come to Christ and live.
    O let his love your hearts constrain,
    nor suffer him to die in vain.

5. This is the time, no more delay!
    This is the Lord's accepted day.
    Come thou, this moment, at his call,
    and live for him who died for all.[2]

Wesley's summons in stanza 2 resounds with God's constant inclusive affirmation: "Ye need not one be left behind" and in stanza 5 with God's inclusive invitation: "Come . . . live for him who died for all." Charles Wesley helps us to see others through God's eyes, to have God's sight and vision. God embraces all through love, the foundation of sharing the Good News of Christ. Simply how we look at others, how our caring demeanor and body language include them with affection will do much to show the power of walking in the way of God's redeeming love in Jesus.

The *Love Feast* creates and evokes the memory that Christ is our guest. He awaits our invitation. He is the stranger born in a stall. He is the refugee child of refugee parents in Egypt. Jesus comes to us often in the Gospels as a stranger needing hospitality. Again Charles Wesley has aptly expressed the motif of our hospitality to Christ in a hymn entitled "The Love Feast."

1. Come, and let us sweetly join,
   Christ to praise in hymns divine;
   give we all with one accord
   glory to our common Lord.

2. Hands and hearts and voices raise,
   sing as in the ancient days;
   antedate the joys above,
   celebrate the feast of love.

3. *Jesus, dear expected Guest,*
   thou art bidden to the feast;
   for thyself our hearts prepare;
   come, and sit, and banquet there.[3]

4. Sanctify us, Lord, and bless,
   breathe thy Spirit, give thy peace;
   thou thyself within us move,
   make our feast a feast of love.

If we wish to share God's Good News of resistless love with others, we will do so when we see with the vision of the Bible, when we see others through God's eyes, as God's own creatures who are for all ages the recipients and objects of God's love. Others sense how you see them. Let them experience the love of Christ through your vision of them. Walter Bruggemann insists: "Our young should be able to perceive, embrace, and enact the word according to the peculiar memory and vision of faith held by the gospel community."[4] For such a community, this vision must be very clear!

Here is what it means to see with God's vision of the Bible:

1. Look where God's eyes look in the world!—beyond the limited vision of self and to the unlikely.
2. Look where the Bible teaches one should look—beyond the community of the faithful.
3. Look where Jesus looked—beyond himself and his own.

Let the way you see others be a powerful testimony of faith in Jesus Christ—that you truly see beyond yourself. Then others will see and sense in you his self-emptying, resistless love.

15. Symbolic Action
Actors in a Drama: Ezekiel 12:1-6

What did the prophet Ezekiel hope to accomplish by packing a bag by daylight for his departure from Jerusalem and then in the evening digging a hole in the wall of the city through which he slipped away into the night with his bag over his shoulder? (See Ezekiel 12:1–6.) His was a symbolic portrayal, a dramatic enactment, of what was going to befall Judah. Her people would be carried away by night into captivity and all they would take with them of their possessions would be what they could carry on their backs. In 596 B.C.E., this is precisely what happened with Judah's overthrow by the Neo-Babylonians.

Through this dramatic depiction of Judah's forthcoming destiny, Ezekiel was witnessing to the reality of God's power and reign in history and to the sinfulness of God's own people, who would be thrust into exile and spread throughout the Fertile Crescent in a diaspora. He was acting out the drama of salvation.

Often the prophets of Israel and Judah delivered ominous words of warning to God's people about the present and future states of their world. They uttered prophetic oracles of hope and doom. To peoples, rulers, and nations they proclaimed God's enduring reign of justice and the futility of human sinfulness and oppression. They spoke eloquently in prose and in poetry. They articulated the hope of God's people for a messiah and painted in word pictures God's vision for humankind in which beauty, peace, truth, justice, purity, and sinlessness reign on earth. Yet, on this occasion, Ezekiel says nothing. Perhaps Ezekiel thought that his actions would speak louder than his words to a people who often turned deaf ears to the words of the prophets.

Ezekiel reminds the contemporary followers of Jesus that the way we consciously choose to act may be a powerful witness to the reality of God's way and truth to others. Does this mean that everyone should consider the possibility of doing what Ezekiel did: plan a dramatic act that will influence a whole city or nation? No, everyone cannot do that. But the prophet does remind us that we must give very careful attention to how we consciously decide to act before others. Our choice of action may symbolize for others the difference between good and bad, meaning and senselessness, life and death.

Our world today is filled with symbolic action. Time and again we have seen television images of terrorists or dissenting groups burning the national flags of countries they oppose for various reasons. We have also seen the flags of Olympic champions raised in tribute as their national anthems are played. At such ceremonies, we have seen African American Olympic champions raise clenched fists in symbolic defiance of racism and affirmation of ethnic identity and justice.

How many communities have tied yellow ribbons around the trees along their streets symbolizing their hope and prayers for the return of loved ones from war and imprisonment?

Some people choose to bless themselves with the sign of the cross as a meaningful act of devotion that witnesses to their life under the sign of the cross. To be sure, the depth of meaning of this is a very personal matter. If such an act becomes mechanical or thought of as having special power in itself, its ultimate meaning is endangered.

Over the doorways to Jewish homes one often sees a *mezuzah,* which contains the Bible verse Deuteronomy 6:4, "Hear, O Israel, the Lord our God is one, the Lord alone." The *mezuzah* symbolizes to all who pass by that this household lives in allegiance to the one true God of Israel.

Christians often wear a cross on a necklace, pin, bracelet, or anklet symbolizing that they live their lives under the sign of the cross of Jesus Christ, the ultimate symbol of self-giving, resistless love. The cross itself has no special power but, when one intentionally elects to wear it, one says to all those with whom one comes in contact, "Here is the model, the pattern for my life for all to see."

Conscious Symbolic Action

We have spoken earlier in this book about how our actions can witness to others when we are unaware of it. In this chapter, however, we are speaking of *conscious* symbolic action and its impact on others. The prophet Ezekiel is very much aware of what he is trying to portray to the people of Judah. His is a conscious dramatic enactment that illustrates what is going to befall Judah. Ezekiel shows a very important aspect of witnessing without words: from time to time we should carefully consider the impact of our actions upon others and judiciously think about how we can best portray our witness through symbolic action. Such action may not always be popular, but the summons to follow Jesus in self-giving, resistless love is not a call to popularity; it is a call to humble service, obedience, and justice.

Conscious symbolic action may be personal. Perhaps one's faithfulness and regularity in prayer, fasting, and meditation will inspire others to a life of faithfulness. When John and Charles Wesley chose to go on a regular basis to the prisons of Oxford with physical and spiritual food for the prisoners, it was an open portrayal of obedience to the servanthood of Christ. It witnessed to the Oxford community that Christians care for the indigent, the convicted, the imprisoned.

It is important to find avenues of conscious, personal, symbolic action. What we do as individuals can powerfully affect the lives of others. This does not mean we have to stand alone. We decide consciously and personally that we will take a stand. It may seem as though we stand alone when what we do requires maintaining integrity against those who are dishonest and have a disregard for truth.

One of my four sons once wore for an extended period of time a large button on his shirt or coat lapel that said, "Question authority!" I used to ask myself, "Is this a plea for anarchy? Is this a desire to obstruct all structure?" As I listened to him over the months and years he wore this button, I began to realize that this was his own symbolic way of saying, "I must truly know for myself that the authority to which I submit has integrity." Authority for authority's sake is itself tyranny. Authority cannot go unquestioned and can only have integrity when it is subjected to scrutiny. In one's early years one accepts the authority of parents, for one depends upon them for existence and survival. But that authority can be, and often is, abused and misused. By my son's symbolic action, the constant button on his shirt or lapel, he was saying to all about him, "Keep the use of authority in proper perspective. Where it is exercised, make certain it has integrity."

The symbols we choose for ourselves send lasting signals of influence to those who surround us. This reality has given birth to an industry of modern-day symbols. To increase interest in their products, numerous companies and corporations today depend on logos, slogans, and symbols. It is big business! Having lived much of my adult life outside the United States, I have become increasingly aware of the kinds of symbols which gain international recognition, such as the "golden arches" or the "swoosh" that adorns caps, shirts, pants, and sports uniforms. But these cannot compare with the symbolic action with which you elect to influence the lives of those around you as a witness to Jesus Christ.

Conscious symbolic action may be corporate. We join in diverse types of corporate symbolic action when we commit ourselves to a common cause with others. The church often witnesses to the gospel of Jesus Christ and his redemptive love without ever uttering a word. Recently I read of a large urban church in Texas whose pastor contacted a local Muslim cleric and worked out an arrangement whereby Christians and Muslims worked side by side in the building of houses for Habitat for Humanity. Such action on the part of Christians is a dramatic enactment of the reality that the God who reclaims life through the Incarnation loves all people, and those who follow the incarnate Christ must also love all people, as God loves them. God's invitation to life and love is to all! It is only as those who accept this invitation personify Christ's selfless and self-giving love, which makes their lives new, that others may be drawn to the same Source of resistless love. Hence, what the corporate life of the church chooses for its symbols in the community where it finds itself and in the world at large will determine in large measure how the gospel of Jesus Christ resonates among the people.

Think of the numerous symbolic acts exercised by Christians and others during the Civil Rights movement in the United States. People formed human chains in defiance of inhumane treatment of African Americans and others. Some simply sat at lunch counters in silent rejection of a system and laws that perpetrated injustice. Dr. Martin Luther King stood for nonviolent protest and elected to act out the drama of injustice by allowing himself to be arrested for the nonviolent breach of laws that supported racial discrimination. These acts were signs or symbols of hope and justice.

There were other symbolic acts in the days of the Civil Rights movement involving hooded figures and burning crosses—symbols of hate and evil. The scenes of bombed and burning African American churches and police dogs attacking opponents of segregation will remain in the memory of the people as symbols of the worst within us—the capacity to hate and to seek resolution through violence, even murder.

It is vitally important that the people who follow Jesus Christ and affirm his gospel of self-giving love choose between the symbols for good and evil and decide, as the body of Christ, the church, to be engaged constantly in acts which symbolize peace, love, justice, kindness, gentleness, meekness, etc. The church itself must be a living symbol of resistless love and solidarity that witnesses in its every act to the enduring healing power of self-emptying love in a world of brokenness, alienation, and pain. The simple act of literally joining hands with those with whom we are least likely to be found joining hands will do much to restore the healing bond of Christian unity.

One of the things which Christians often do during a service of worship is to "pass the peace" or to "show signs of peace" to one another. Often they embrace or clasp hands and say simply, "Peace be with you," or "The peace of Christ be with you." Here is a conscious, corporate symbolic act that is worth holding before the world as a symbol of what the church of Jesus Christ really is: the fellowship of God's people extending their hands to one another and everyone throughout God's creation and demonstrating in everything they do that they are instruments of Christ's peace. They say to everyone: "The peace of Christ be with you," and they seek the realization of this peace in their own lives and those of others.

We are all actors in the drama of salvation. How well will you play the part of a committed, loving witness of Christ?

16. Finding the Balance

One speaks of the Christian church as the "community of faith." It is not generally referred to as the "community of proclaimers." It is not simply a community of "evangelists," though it might be called a "community of evangels," one in which everyone's life proclaims that self-giving, resistless love in community, as expressed in Jesus Christ, is the path to true identity.

How does one evangelize the community and the person in community? *First of all, one must rethink the idea that evangelism is merely a verbal act of proclaiming God's Good News to others. We witness with our lives!* Community assumes relationship. Community is based upon the reality that a person can only be a person in relationship, in community. Human beings were created as a part of God's creation, not merely as creatures within nature. They were created for relationship to one another *and* to the whole of creation. Walter Bruggemann states: "The victory of God over death is not a victory over some selected zones of life, but over all creation and against every threat of chaos."[1] Therefore, any viable understanding of evangelization, which proclaims God's victory over death in Christ, must begin from the premise that relationship to God the Creator, creation, and all God's creatures is the foundation of all life, personhood, and community. The proclamation of the Good News of Jesus Christ cannot have integrity without the establishment of these relationships. "Evangelism" as often practiced has sometimes left the impression that as long as one's relationship with God is "established" or "made right," nothing else matters and all God desires to know is that one is a repentant sinner who trusts in the redemptive love of the divine Son, Jesus Christ. Not so, according to the Holy Scriptures. There is no relationship with God without a wholesome and reconciled relationship with others and creation. The New Testament teaches that there is no greater love than this—that you lay down your life for your friend. The Bible also teaches that the whole of creation groans for redemption. If one takes the Scriptures at face value, the love of God, love of others, and love of all creation are mutually inclusive, not mutually exclusive.

The proclamation of the Good News of Jesus Christ can have little lasting value without the establishment of community—relationship. It is possible to establish a plethora of contacts but no relationships. There will always be a creative tension between personal and social loyalties, between personal freedom and social responsibility. But it is not enough simply to know one's identity; there must be continuity in one's life.

Secondly, to have integrity, evangelization must be based upon continuity, which takes place within community. People live within a web of promises, and the keeping of promises to one another establishes trust, the foundation of continuity. One discovers true identity among those whom one trusts. It is here that one finds the nexus of verbal and nonverbal evangelism. It is impossible to have one without the other. The verbal proclamation of the Good News of Jesus Christ must be translated into relationships. The Good News must be experienced through trust among those who exemplify that the self-giving love of Jesus on the cross transforms individuals into community with lasting relationships, mutual trust, and, hence, true identity and continuity. If you keep the promise to love others as God has loved you, you will gain trust. Break your promises to others and you will destroy trust and lose identity.

Thirdly, relationship in God's community does not mean merely relationship to others but rather to all of God's creation. Is God truly the God of history? Yes, and the community of the faithful experiences nature as God's creation. There is no "human" history apart from "creation" history. However, this is not to imply, in some pantheistic sense, that human beings are a "part of nature" *per se;* rather, according to the Bible, a person's true identity is realized in the community of faith in relationship to God, others, and the whole of God's creation. The earth itself in its process of regeneration patterns our life in creation. We too are in need of regeneration.

What happens after conversion and regeneration, after acceptance of God's self-giving love in Jesus Christ as the basis for one's life in community? One's relationship to God, others, and creation is changed. One is reconciled to the whole—to God, others, *and* the whole of creation. One seeks then to live out a trust relationship within community, in harmony within and with creation. It is perhaps easier to measure this in human relationships, because one responds to others and one is responded to by others. Often the inanimate parts of creation seem depersonalized and, hence, human beings tend to misuse them. But the Scriptures tell us that all creation groans for redemption. Misuse of the resources that sustain creation only widens the breach between human beings and the world God has made. Wherever there is no reconciliation in God's creation, the Good News of Jesus Christ has not been heard. Wherever creation has been exploited, evangelization desperately needs to take place. And the church, the community of faith, must lead this process, be it in verbal or nonverbal witness.

Just after the fall of the Berlin wall in November 1989, I drove with a friend from Nürnberg, Germany, to Berlin. All along the highway in what had been East Germany (the German Democratic Republic, DDR) the trees were blackened with soot from the burning of brown coal, and, as one looked across the fields on both sides of the road, a heavy cloud of smog hung above them. I thought to myself, "All creation is groaning today for healing and reconciliation. It too desires to be the recipient of self-giving, redemptive love." Just as those who are forsaken may look to the forsaken One on the cross and know they are not alone—that there is someone who is in solidarity with them—so God's creation yearns in its forsakenness for the same reconciling, self-emptying love to heal its wounds and to be in solidarity with a forsaken creation—the earth, the sky, and all that is.

The Balance

How can we find the balance between verbal and wordless witnessing to Jesus' resistless love? How do we balance evangelistic proclamation, filled with the rich biblical message of the human condition and God's redeeming love, and *diakonia,* ministries of service that live out the Good News? How do we witness with our lives? How do we become resistless love? There are many who view evangelism as the proclamation of the content of the Christian faith and the activities of evangelism as including preaching, personal witnessing, writing, and employment of the media and other avenues of

communication. The stress here is on the utterance of the gospel message. Others view *diakonia* as sufficient articulation of the Good
News. When these two are polarized, those who do so miss the mark
of holy scripture, which does not create an "either/or" choice. The
polarization was created by human beings, not God.

What then is binding from scripture as regards the proclamation
of the Good News of Jesus Christ? James C. Logan points out in
Theology and Evangelism in the Wesleyan Heritage that the priority
given to the Great Commission must be evaluated in the light of the
history of the Christian faith. It was not the central focus of the
Reformers. Rather, the

> Anabaptists were the first to make the commission
> mandatory for all believers. The person really to be cred-
> ited with putting it on the map, so to speak, was William
> Carey in his 1792 tract entitled *An Enquiry into the
> Obligations of Christians to Use Means for the
> Conversion of the Heathen,* in which he, with the aid of a
> simple yet powerful argument, demolished the conven-
> tional Reformation interpretation of Matthew 28:18–20.
> In other words, aside from the Anabaptists, the Great
> Commission did not have wide currency until the modern
> world missionary movement began in the late eighteenth
> century.[2]

What does this say about the witness of the church for eighteen centuries? The gospel spread, lives were changed, the church grew, faith
did not die, even without a central emphasis on Matthew 28.

Once again, no case is made in this book for diminishing the vital
verbal witness. Rather, it makes a plea for a larger understanding of
what it means to *declare* the Good News of Jesus Christ in the whole
of one's life. Charles Wesley's lines quoted in the "Introduction" of
this work do not fit a definition of Christian proclamation which
avers that "Proclamation is only distinctively Christian communication insofar as it is both uttered and listened to in faith."[3] Note once
more Wesley's lines about Elizabeth Blackwell.

> By wisdom pure and peaceable,
> by the meek Spirit of the Lord,

she knows the stoutest to compel,
and sinners wins without the word:
they see the tempers of the Lamb,
and bow subdued to Jesu's name,
as captives of resistless love.

Is Charles Wesley simply wrong? A primary goal of evangelization is to win sinners, but can you do it "without the word"? According to Wesley, the answer is yes! Of course, he means the "spoken word." You can so bear the tempers of the Lamb of God in your body, in your being, that others become captives of the resistless love of Jesus you have come to know and live.

Here we find a hallmark of the theology of the Wesleys. They believed that life rooted in love, God's self-giving, self-emptying love, can change lives. In this way, one understands grace to be active and dynamic, with power to convert and evoke change. Grace is multidimensional. "The Wesleyan heritage in its earliest days possessed a grasp of the wholeness of the gospel as grace active in mission." Therefore, "if we act as instruments of God's grace—lives can be changed by grace."[4] This is precisely what Charles Wesley celebrates in the life of Elizabeth Blackwell. She had learned to live, to act as an instrument of grace. Wesley himself had observed that this was precisely the reason that persons with the most resistance to the gospel, "the stoutest," bowed "subdued to Jesu's name" through her witness "without the word." She lived her witness!

"Resistless love" is a vital key to the Wesleyan theology of evangelization. One finds a balance between faith recognition and experience, between "knowing" and "feeling," by "being rooted and grounded in love" (Ephesians 3:17–18). One is able to "comprehend" the depth of God's love and to "know" such love in and through one's experience, because one is "rooted and grounded in love." Love alone provides the balance between nonverbal and verbal witnessing. Love alone fills one "with all the fullness of God." One preaches Christ (1 Corinthians 1:23) in all one does. This means that one's life is filled with *kerygmatic* content—the heart of the gospel message is personified in one's life.

This does not mean one can substitute witnessing without words for witnessing with words. But it does mean that, if one excludes from evangelism dimensions of Christian living and Christian ministry which, as Charles Wesley has emphasized, can convert and bring regeneration to the lives of others, one has missed the spirit of the Holy Scriptures; for the Bible does not provide a unilinear definition of "evangelism." While social ministries of the church *cannot* substitute for witnessing with words, to exclude social ministries from evangelization in order to prevent the watering down of "true evangelism" is a refusal to admit what Charles Wesley declared is a reality. You can so embody, so dimension the reality of faith and self-emptying love in your life that others will make the decision to become followers of Jesus.

Hence, a sense of balance in evangelization demands that we become more sensitive to the wholeness of the mandates of the Scriptures regarding spreading the Good News. Such a balance requires a new look at *diakonia*. There is nothing the church does in mission which does not have implications for evangelization. Love provides the balance.

Does *diakonia* only have integrity if it is the context for evangelistic proclamation? Love does not allow for an affirmative response to this question, for Jesus shows how loving service is Good News personified. Is *diakonia* then simply a good thing which has its place in Christian living, but is not to be designated as evangelization? While *diakonia* cannot be a substitute for *witnessing with words,* Charles Wesley maintains you can create an atmosphere of resistless love in whatever you do such that others are drawn to Jesus Christ. It is here that the church in the present and future needs to do considerable "soul searching" in reference to its many ministries of mission. It needs a new and careful look at what it means to create an atmosphere of the resistless love of Jesus Christ through ministries of service, *diakonia.* This was a self-understood imperative which undergirded the revival of the Wesleys in the eighteenth century. It is an imperative that needs to be rediscovered by the church at the end of the twentieth century and in the new millennium.

There are many contexts in our world today where silent faithfulness may be the strongest proclamation one can make for Jesus Christ. G. Howard Mellor avers: "The only way that some people are going to hear the good news of Jesus is if someone goes to them and creates friends amongst those of other cultures and tenets."[5]

Endnotes

1. The Witness of Evangelical Word and Presence
1. Personal correspondence, January 17, 2000.
2. Samuel Hugh Moffett *A History of Christianity in Asia,* Vol. 1 (New York: Harper San Francisco, 1992), p. xiii.
3. Walter Bruggemann, *Biblical Perspectives on Evangelism* (Nashville: Abingdon, 1993), p. 13.
4. Albert Outler, *Evangelism in the Wesleyan Spirit* (Nashville: Discipleship Resources, 1996), p. 22.
5. Priscilla Pope-Levison, "Is a Holistic Evangelism Possible?" in Russell E. Richey, William B. Lawrence, Dennis M. Campbell, eds., *Questions for the Twenty-First Century* (Nashville: Abingdon Press, 1999), p. 40.

3. The Witness of Resistless Love
1. Cervantes in *Man of La Mancha,* a musical play by Dale Wassermann, Joe Darian, and Mitch Leigh (New York: Random House, 1966), pp. 60–61.
2. Stanza one of a hymn by Anna B. Warner, 1859.
3. The leading character of the play of the same name by Edmond Rostand.
4. See *The Unpublished Poetry of Charles Wesley,* 3 vols., edited by S T Kimbrough, Jr., and Oliver A. Beckerlegge (Nashville: Kingswood /Abingdon, 1990), 2: 404.
5. Charles Wesley, *Hymns for the Nativity of our Lord* (Bristol: Farley, 1745).
6. Petros Vassiliadis, *Eucharist and Witness: Orthodox Perspectives on the United Mission of the Church* (Geneva: WCC Publications, 1996), p. 43.

4. The Witness of Evangelizing Love
1. Charles Wesley, *Hymns and Sacred Poems* (Bristol: Farley, 1742), p. 119.
2. By "plastic power," Wesley means God's formative, creative power.
3. Charles Wesley, *Hymns of Petition and Thanksgiving for the Promise of the Father* (Bristol: Farley, 1746), No. 28, p. 31.
4. Orlando Costas, *Liberating News* (Grand Rapids, MI: William B. Eerdmans, 1989), p. 21.
5. Walter Bruggemann, *Biblical Perspectives on Evangelism* (Nashville: Abingdon, 1993), p. 115.
6. *Ibid.,* see p. 44.

5. The Witness of Holy Communion
1. See *The United Methodist Hymnal* (Nashville: United Methodist Publishing House, 1989), Hymn 616, stanzas 2-4.

2. Petros Vassiliadis, *Eucharist and Witness*, p. 53.
3. *The United Methodist Hymnal* (1989), Hymn 616, stanza 1.
4. *The United Methodist Hymnal,* (Nashville: United Methodist Publishing House, 1989), p. 10.

6. Mustard Seed

1. The Methodist Episcopal Church, South, the Methodist Episcopal Church, and the Methodist Protestant Church united in 1939 to form The Methodist Church, hence, the name was officially changed in Lithuania as well.
2. This is the author's English translation of the first four lines of the German hymn "Die Sach' ist dein, Herr Jesu Christ."

7. Light

1. *The Methodist Hymnal* (Nashville: The Methodist Publishing House, 1966), Hymn 272.
2. *Ibid.,* Hymn 148.
3. Charles Wesley, *Hymns for Children,* No. 29; see Osborn, *The Poetical Works of John and Charles Wesley* (1878), 6:392–93.
4. *Hymns and Sacred Poems* (1739), p.117.
5. Albert Outler, *Evangelism in the Wesleyan Spirit* (Nashville: Discipleship Resources, 1996), p. 22.
6. *Ibid.,* Matthew 5:14–15.
7. *The United Methodist Hymnal* (1989), Hymn 183, stanza 3.
8. *Ibid.,* stanzas 1, 2, 4.

8. Salt

1. John Wesley, *Explanatory Notes Upon the New Testament* (Grand Rapids: Baker Bookhouse, 1986; originally published in London 1755), Matthew 5:13-15.

12. Shadows

1. *Abingdon Bible Commentary* (Nashville: Abingdon Press, 1959), p. 568.

13. Justice and Piety

1. A paraphrase by this author. The refrain is from Micah 6:8.
2. Stanza 1 of a hymn by Charles Wesley found at the conclusion of a pamphlet by John Wesley entitled *A Short View of the Differences between the Moravian Brethren, Lately in England, and the Rev. Mr. John and Charles Wesley* (1748). Stanzas 2 and 3 are included in *The United Methodist Hymnal (1989);* see Hymn 635.

14. Beyond Ourselves
1. Daniel L. Migliore, "Christology in Context," *Interpretation* 40 (1995), p. 252.
2. See *The United Methodist Hymnal* (1989), Hymn 339.
3. The italics are this author's addition. See *The United Methodist Hymnal* (1989), Hymn 699.
4. Walter Bruggemann, *Biblical Perspectives on Evangelism* (Nashville: Abingdon, 1993), p. 98.

16. Finding the Balance
1. Bruggemann (1993), p. 44.
2. James C. Logan, editor, *Theology and Evangelism in the Wesleyan Heritage* (Nashville: Abingdon, 1994); see his chapter: "The Evangelical Imperative: A Wesleyan Perspective," p. 21.
3. Lewis A. Drummond, *The Word of the Cross: A Contemporary Theology of Evangelism* (Nashville: Broadman, 1992), p. 217.
4. Logan, "The Evangelical Imperative: A Wesleyan Perspective," in Logan (1994), p. 20.
5. G. Howard Mellor, "Evangelism and Religious Pluralism in the Wesleyan Heritage," in Logan (1994), p. 123.

 **S T Kimbrough, Jr.,** is a native of Alabama and a member of the North Alabama Conference of The United Methodist Church. He holds a doctorate in Old Testament and Semitic languages from Princeton Theological Seminary and is a graduate of Birmingham Southern College and the Divinity School of Duke University. Dr. Kimbrough is an internationally known scholar/ musician who has published over twenty books and numerous articles on biblical, theological, liturgical, musical, and Wesleyan subjects, and has performed and recorded widely throughout Europe and the United States. Currently Associate General Secretary for Mission Evangelism of the General Board of Global Ministries of The United Methodist Church, he has served churches in Alabama, North Carolina, New Jersey, and Germany.

Dr. Kimbrough has also taught on leading theological and university faculties in the US and abroad, including Princeton Theological Seminary, Friedrich Wilhelm University of Bonn, Germany, New Brunswick Theological Seminary, and the Illiricus Theological Faculty of Zagreb (formerly Yugoslavia). He has also been a member of the Center of Theological Inquiry in Princeton, New Jersey. While at the center, he organized the first international colloquium of scholars on Charles Wesley Studies and subsequently organized the Charles Wesley Society, serving as its first president.

A specialist in Charles Wesley studies, he has devoted years of study to Charles Wesley's life and works. He is author/editor of the following books: *The Old Testament as the Book of Christ* (Westminster Press, 1976, translation), *Israelite Religion in Sociological Perspective* (Harrassowitz, 1978), *Lost in Wonder: The Meaning of Charles Wesley's Hymns for Today* (Upper Room Books, 1987), *Sweet Singer* (Hinshaw Music, Inc., 1987, vocal arrangements of Wesley hymns), *The Unpublished Poetry of Charles Wesley*, 3 vols., coedited with Oliver A. Beckerlegge (Kingswood, 1988, 1990, 1992), *Charles Wesley: Poet and Theologian* (Kingswood, 1992), *Psalms for Praise and Worship* (Abingdon, 1992), *A Song for the Poor* (GBGM, 1993, Charles Wesley hymns for ministry with the poor), *A Heart to Praise My God* (Abingdon, 1996, a commentary on the Wesley hymns in the 1989 *United Methodist Hymnal*), and *Methodism in Russia and the Baltic States: History and Renewal* (1995). He was a member of the Wesley Consultation for the 1989 *United Methodist Hymnal*, as well as one of the editors of its liturgical psalter. The musical drama *Sweet Singer*, which he wrote and premiered at New York's Carnegie Hall in 1985, has been performed by him throughout the US, Europe, and Asia.

Order all resources by stock number from the Service Center.
Please mail order with check payable to:
SERVICE CENTER
P.O. BOX 691328
CINCINNATI, OH 45269-1328

COSTS FOR SHIPPING
AND HANDLING:

Sale Items:
$25 or less, add $3.50
$25.01-$60 add $4.50
$60.01-$100, add $5.50
Over $100, add 5%

For billed or credit card orders
CALL TOLL FREE: 1-800-305-9857 FAX ORDERS: 1-513-761-3722
If billing is requested, $1.50 billing fee is charged.
Mail to: SERVICE CENTER, GENERAL BOARD OF GLOBAL MINISTRIES,
THE UNITED METHODIST CHURCH, 7820 READING RD. CALLER NO. 1800
CINCINNATI, OH 45222-1800

Price $7.95   4/00   Recycled Paper (ECF)   Stock #2846